THE OXFORD ANTHOLOGY OF

# Bhakti
## *literature*

THE OXFORD ANTHOLOGY OF

# Bhakti
## *literature*

*edited by*
Andrew Schelling

OXFORD
UNIVERSITY PRESS

# OXFORD
UNIVERSITY PRESS

Oxford University Press is a department of the University of Oxford.
It furthers the University's objective of excellence in research, scholarship,
and education by publishing worldwide. Oxford is a registered trademark of
Oxford University Press in the UK and in certain other countries

Published in India
by Oxford University Press
YMCA Library Building, Jai Singh Road, New Delhi 110 001, India

ISBN-13: 978-0-19-806912-6
ISBN-10: 0-19-806912-X

Typeset in Adobe Garamond Pro 10.5/12.5
by Sai Graphic Design, New Delhi 110 055
Printed in India at Rakmo Press, New Delhi 110 020

*The mountain throws a shadow,*
*Thin is the moon's horn;*
*What did we remember*
*Under the ragged thorn?*
*Dread has followed longing,*
*And our hearts are torn.*

—William Butler Yeats

*It is an absorbing tale of an illness*
*that does not end in the grave*

—Chandidas

# Contents

# Acknowledgements

Ira Raja first approached me about a pan-Indian bhakti book. Her patient, studied conviction helped me see it could be done by a poet who held few credentials as a scholar and who lived in a far-off country. Conversations with her in Delhi, in Colorado, by phone, and by email, have kept me on track for three years. Among other friends from India, I want specifically to thank *thumri* singer Vidya Rao, as well as Raji Ramanujan, Prabodh Parikh, and Dilip Chitre. All provided generous thoughts along the way. Bob and Susan Arnold in Brattleboro, Vermont, responded to some of my own translations by rapidly producing little editions of Lal Ded and Dadu. Lengthy discussions about book-making, manuscripts, poetry, local technology, and India's vernacular traditions with printer and book designer Ken Botnick have been nothing short of breathtaking. Conversations with botanist Tim Hogan on the mountain trails of Colorado helped me formulate thoughts about the 'natural habitat' of the bhakti poem, and the structure of this collection.

The anthologies and writings of Jerome Rothenberg were indispensable to my own work, and the writings on oral tradition by Barbara and Dennis Tedlock, Robert Bringhurst, Dell Hymes, and other colleagues have been instrumental to my thinking. Those scholars let many of the translation dragons out of the box, for which I am endlessly grateful. Kristen Anderson helpfully critiqued some of this book. Kabir Chaitanya patiently guided me in an effort to learn some raga singing. Althea Schelling listened just as patiently to my singing as well as to my wildest ideas. And Marlow Brooks provided spiritual insight, candid thoughts, unswerving support, and infectious enthusiasm when I most needed it.

In the end, my deepest gratitude goes to the original singers, the sacred poets, who risked themselves on every word that has ended up here. They held the visions, often in the teeth of contempt, ridicule, expulsion, or violence. They sang, chanted, mewled, growled, yawped, and in the end crafted the first words and the original music, passing it on to people they would never know. This book is for them.

May 2011                                          Andrew Schelling

# Introduction

## Migration

As the last of the bhakti poems finds its place in this volume, and the book's final structure rounds into shape, a hard March wind drives snow down from the western peaks of Colorado. It carves ravines and whorls of ice about the log cabin, and a snowdrift rises over the north window. This cabin sits in a valley of soaring rock-walls honeycombed with mines from the gold and silver rushes of the nineteenth century. Before that, the archaeological record shows, this valley has served as a migration road and trade route for 10,000 years or longer—since the last glaciation.

If this ecozone at 3,000 metres elevation, with its bare rock, stiff tundra, and bitingly cold creek, seems far from Tamil Nadu's villages, the scrubby sun-bitten hills of Rajasthan, or Bengal's watercourses, that is precisely my reason for invoking it. The specific cultural, intellectual, economic, and emotional factors within bhakti poetry remain distinct to South Asia, and the greatest temptation for modern, literate people is to assume its emotions, aspirations, or lyric forms are readily accessible to educated residents across the planet. A workable library of bhakti does have its place in Colorado's high valleys though, if only for the fact that an international readership, or audience of listeners, has grown up around the lyrics of Kabir, Mirabai, Antal, and Vidyapati during the past century.

The poems of the bhakti tradition began to take shape in India during the eighth or ninth centuries. Scholars have tracked its origins in *Svetasvatara Upanishad*, Bhagavadgita, *Bhagavata Purana*, and other texts that advocate or describe the yoga of devotion. At this point we can document the names of hundreds, if not thousands of singers who fit the profile of bhakti. These poets have been drawn largely from the old excluded orders of India's political or social hierarchies, and their songs and subversive beliefs caused upheavals in families and entire clans. At times, revolutions spread across whole kingdoms, propelled by the emotions of bhakti. Driven by spiritual hunger, a fierce desire for spiritual freedom, and long-simmering demands for social or economic equality, bhakti poets issued forth in dozens of languages. Though few of the longings they articulate feel alien to this Colorado valley from which I write, bhakti is salted with an intensity that requires intellectual effort and a great deal of honest probing to get close to.

At the root of bhakti coils the formidable old hunger for human freedom, a sense of the world's inexplicable mystery, and the conviction that each of us forms some personal relationship to that mystery. As a North American poet, I find parallels in Native American vision quest songs, in African-American gospel, the blues, labour protest songs, and most significantly in my own 'tradition'—the experimental and liberatory impulses of international modernist and postmodern poetry.

At the same time I want to resist any impulse to try a quick assimilation. Fifteen years ago, when I published a book of translations of the sixteenth-century bhakta Mirabai, the American poet and anthropologist Nathaniel Tarn wrote to me. How, he asked, could a person live their whole life on such an edge? So perilously in love with an unattainable beloved? How could she maintain the tension of her ferocious unrequited love for Krishna for decades? While the emotion itself may seem familiar, its duration and intensity locate it in a realm of experience not easily reached.

There is an essay the North American poet Kenneth Rexroth wrote during worldwide political upheavals in the 1960s, in which he defined the 'counterculture' as 'those people who live by the tenets of lyric poetry'. This would be a suitable place to start talking about bhakti. What sets the poets of bhakti apart from their classical Sanskrit or Tamil predecessors—transforming them into a prominent *countercultural* force—is their resolve to match life and poetry: To live by what they sing, no matter the stakes. Some bhakti poets gathered around themselves 'communities of dissent' in their own lifetimes. As much as they drew from the traditions of India—both the so-called 'Great' and the so-called 'Little Traditions'—the passions given speech in their poems were designed to shatter any fetters of belief that would limit the ferocity of experience.

Uncritically placing bhakti poets alongside singers in far-off traditions inadvertently does just that: it limits the intensity of the living poem.

The editors of a very different sort of anthology, a collection of contemporary avant-garde poets of the British Isles, use words I think helpful:

It is important to remember here that tradition, as instrument of power, sanctions agreed habits of syntax, rhythms and sequences of thought, intonation, figurative language, and range of diction. The normative impulses of literary and linguistic tradition reinforce notions of intelligibility (and of syntax) ... Its vocabulary prizes terms like 'unified' and 'centered', for in proposing their contraries—edges, margins, fragments—such terms trivialize and thus silent dissent. (Caddel and Quartermain, *Other*)

What I want to get at is this: at a level deeper than what a poem or song *says*, occur disruptions or subversions that appear both spiritual and linguistic. These include forbidden emotions, raw vernacular vocabulary, riddles, secret codes, and non-rational images. There is also a question of context: the disruptive force of speech, prayer, liturgy, or song when used by people who have been forbidden it.

When the editors at Oxford University Press approached me about an anthology in English translation of bhakti poetry, I resisted at first. I have some facility in Sanskrit—thirty off-and-on years as a translator, with excursions into Hindi, Pali, and some of the Prakrits. But my life has been lived as an American poet. Better, I thought, someone who knows a good number of the languages, and knows them well. Someone who inhabits from birth the range of India's cultures, and can approach bhakti from an indigenous point of view. Someone who has come of age among the traditions and counter-traditions in question.

What I came to see though, through that swarm of first doubts, was this: to regard bhakti as a religious emotion locked inside India, or to fret over the supposed impenetrability of the languages and cultures in which bhakti appears, is to diminish its poets. It is to pretend that those singers were parochial figures, understandable by, or of interest to, only a small local audience. In fact the greatest poets of bhakti—and there are many, far more than this book can accommodate—stand with the bravest poets across our planet. Their songs have migrated not just across India, but also into Europe and the Americas. They are collaborators in the effort to find the dimensions of the human heart and mind, and to readjust the world we live in—to wrench or crack it open—so we might drop old prejudice. Rather than think the poets fenced in by languages tough for an outsider to approach—Tamil, Telugu, Bengali, or the Braj Bhasha dialect—why not observe that through the attentive work of translators, such poets may visit villages far from their own?

Forty years ago the American poet Robert Duncan wrote that the work of our own times was to convoke a 'symposium of the whole' in which 'all the old excluded orders must be included'. 'The female, the proletariat, the foreign; the animal and vegetative; the unconscious and the unknown; the criminal and failure—all that has been outcast and vagabond must return to be admitted into the creation of what we consider we are.'

I can think of no better point of orientation than Duncan's call, as a gate or entry to the range of bhakti poetry.

## Origins

About 2,500 years ago the word bhakti surfaced in India. It appears in *Svetasvatara Upanishad* and in the Bhagavadgita, a term that denotes love or devotion directed to a deity or a god. *Bhava madbhakto*, says Krishna: Be my devotee. The word derives from the Sanskrit verb *bhaj*, which initially meant to divide, share, or distribute. Over time, the verb came to mean partake, enjoy, participate; to eat, to make love. From such personal colourings it took abstract meanings. To experience, to feel, to adore; to serve, honour, or worship. There is also a noun, *bhakta*, meaning a votary, a worshipper, a lover.

The diverse traditions of yoga, meanwhile, extended the devotional type of love known as bhakti to include in its reach holy persons or spiritual teachers. For several thousand years bhakti has been regarded as one among many paths to spiritual realization, along with *jnana, karma,* and other disciplines suited to individual temper. But something new appeared around 1,200 years ago, taking shape first in Tamil country. This new expression understood bhakti as the singular path, and in many instances the only appropriate path to liberation. Instead of a quiet, reflective approach to a deity, it generated a passionate, unyielding, and existentialist attitude to the devotee's own experience. This has meant a devotion that is strikingly personal, scornful of hand-me-down doctrine, unwilling to entrust oneself to the hands of priests or state-sanctioned religions. Most importantly, it locates spiritual truth in the body and heart of the worshipper. Rather than suppressing uncertainty, longing, or desire, it embraces them. Immersion in the physical body and its stormy emotions leads the bhakta away from theory, theology, doctrine, or elaborate metaphysics; it draws him or her into realms of dance, poetry, and song.

## Histories

Bhakti poetry occurs at the confluence of Sanskrit with India's vernacular traditions. It also exceeds the reach of either. Its first singular emergence—the point at which most scholars name the appearance of something radically new—occurred in Tamil Nadu, around the eighth or ninth century. Its poems took shape in Tamil language. The new vision drew on pan-Indian themes, collecting inspiration from Sanskrit tradition, local vernacular cultures, and classical Tamil literature, though in many ways its impulse was subversive of each of these. Bhakti, and the poems that convey its passions, are, in A.K. Ramanujan's words, deliberately 'anti-tradition'.

That first upheaval, in Tamil Nadu, set many of bhakti's terms—defiance of ritual and orthodoxy; rejection of educated speech or stylized metrics; a turning away from classical training in poetics. In imagery, rhythm, and idiom, bhakti poems sound strikingly modern, with a thrust towards illogic, distinctly personal voices pressing up through often troubling imagery. A 'dark, ambiguous language of ciphers', writes Ramanujan of some of the poems, and quotes Mircea Eliade: 'analogies, homologies, and double meanings'. Lest anyone consider such poems mere riddles, I want to stress that behind every poem you hear is sharply articulated conflict, the struggles of a living person questioning his or her own experience in native speech. Regularly that speech manages to force new openings into language, disrupting conventional patterns of image-making or syntax. Unlike most scriptures or religious verse, in bhakti the poem's emotion and its drama stay focused on the poet. They are rarely simple praise poems to a deity. Rarely do they attempt metaphysical assertion. Much more do they speak to a relationship as tumultuous as that between two human beings.

Over the course of a thousand years (measuring from eighth- or ninth-century Tamil Nadu), bhakti took shape in India's west, then spread across the north, and eventually surged forth in the eastern regions of Bengal and Orissa. A Sanskrit saying runs,

> Bhakti took birth in Dravidian lands
> ripened in Karnataka, came to
> womanhood in Maharashtra, and grew
> crone-like in Gujarat.
> Reaching Vrindavana she re-emerged
> a nubile young woman.

This clockwise 'maturation' and renewal around India, beginning in the south, does not mean that bhakti simply passed from region to region, nor that it spread in an easily charted chronology. It also does not mean—despite the Sanskrit verse's implication—that it maintains one single identity.

If religious orthodoxy takes a few standardized or prescribed forms, then the efforts to break free of social constraint are never standard or predictable, and took hundreds of forms in India. Scholars and poets have examined some of the historical conditions for bhakti. There is little use in my repeating here the hard work done in books and articles by Lorenzen, Ramanujan, Hawley, and others. I refer interested readers to this collection's bibliography. The principal poets who come down to us look wild, untutored, often quite mad from the standpoint of conventional social norms. Try to generalize about their beliefs, and some hectoring poet will show up with a contradictory phrase, a puzzling stanza, or a swift image that confounds any earlier assumption.

## What is a Bhakti Poem?

Bhakti poetry begins in the human voice. Its poems are to be spoken, sung, or chanted. Dilip Chitre (1938–2009), who had worked extensively with the Varkari tradition of Maharashtra, uses a term I find helpful: orature. In almost every instance, bhakti is oral poetry, orature not literature, enunciated by the poet, and written onto the page only later—often centuries later. In this sense its natural habitat has always been performance.

This means that a translation, printed on the page, will generally show only part of what the poem is: the linguistic elements. And of those, largely the elements that seem to be 'meaningful'. Translation often cannot replicate tones of speech, the steep climbs and ornamental descents of the singer's voice, the repetition of words and phrases; it cannot do justice to vocal sounds that hold no fixed meanings, or to words that undergo deliberate or ritual distortion. The presence of subterranean and folk traditions throughout India, magical or mystical in nature, should alert us to the possibility that the most important part of a song may not be 'what it says'. Magical language-use occurs among all tribal and non-literate people; traditions such as yoga and tantra cultivate the paradox and the echo, even inventing initiatory or secret languages-within-language.

When Kabir in one poem claims he speaks the eastern dialect, and people of the west do not get his meaning, he may be referring to more than shifts of pronunciation across geographic regions. A long tradition of secret languages exists in India—known in Sanskrit as *sandhya-bhasa* (or *sandha-bhasa*), twilight speech or intentional speech. A 'process of destroying and reinventing language can be observed', writes Mircea Eliade in *Yoga: Immortality and Freedom*. These traditions, he goes on, 'are composed in … a secret, dark, ambiguous language in which a state of consciousness is expressed' (Eliade 1958: 249).

American poet Archibald MacLeish (1892–1982) famously wrote, 'A poem should not mean but be.' You could say traditions of magic and spiritual inquiry are more interested in what a poem *does* than what it means. 'What a poem does', though—if the poem emerged in an oral culture and intends to 'project the yogin' (Eliade) into a particular state of awareness, or to contact the spirits or a deity—is hard to get from the printed page. Not impossible to get, but differently arrived at. My intention, as I compiled this anthology, was to search for and present translations that come near to what a poem does. This means I have at times bypassed celebrated or 'central' figures—especially those translated from a sectarian point of view—in favour of lesser-known poets or poems that hit harder today, because they hold more of that ambiguous dark speech. Some will be poets who have luckily found a capable translator—a translator who has worked to instil the echoes, ambiguities, or other non-semantic procedures of poetry. This I want to acknowledge ahead of time, for anyone who might complain that I have elevated peripheral figures or bypassed canonical poets.

In this context I need to point out that bhakti typically existed away from the centres of power. Reading poetry that holds a religious or spiritual charge, we need to remain alert to how the old poetry may have been distorted or corrupted to serve the ends of sectarian religions, ethnic exclusion, or nationalism. Oral poetries have no state to protect them and no high technology (such as writing) to solidify or render them incorruptible. They remain vulnerable—not just to change, which is part of their living condition—but to manipulation.

Certainly the accounts of the lives of bhakti poets carry layers of added-on story, later accretions that take low caste or outcaste poets and 'brahminize' them, provide them with fabulous births, or a guru who is properly orthodox, and otherwise distort their heritage. If the life stories undergo this kind of pressure, there can be no doubt that songs have been subject to similar restatement. Later assimilation to powerful creeds, recognition of individual poets by kings or emperors, or the development of sectarian groups around dead poets, can leave us moderns with a skewed sense of what held power, *shakti*, for the first audiences.

## The Six Roads of Bhakti Poetry

Because this is an anthology of printed material, I am going to draw up some characteristics of a bhakti poem worth keeping in mind. I have reworked certain features pointed out by American poet Jerome Rothenberg in the 1968 collection, *Technicians of the Sacred: A Range of Poetries from Africa, America, Asia, Europe and Oceania* edited by him. Rothenberg, at the time wanted to outline fertile intersections between 'primitive poetry' and modern avant-garde practice. He was providing contemporary poets with a raw sense of how the past can inform the present, and he looked to create 'lines of recovery and discovery'. Shifting and compressing Rothenberg's observations, I have located six features—I would like to call them roads—that address what goes on with a bhakti poem.

1. The poem is carried by the poet's voice. It has been composed orally, sometimes spontaneously. Only later has it been written down. Frequently, its models (sources of inspiration, or of musical or metrical form) were local folk traditions. The full range of vocal sound may be employed, along with instrumental music. The poem is to be recited, intoned, sung, and chanted. No two presentations will sound the same, and the order of images or 'lines' would not necessarily have been fixed. Contemporary singers are a good guide to the fluid order of lines and images. Reading a bhakti poem, keep the drum skin close to hand.

2. A highly-developed process of thinking in images. Often these images are built on polarities, or held tense by conflict. Contradiction, illogic, paradox, non-causal thought—all are techniques deliberately used by the poet. Narrative comes in bright, sharp image, and personal cries, not through plot or storytelling. Consistent emotions are rarely held. 'You say I contradict myself? Very well, I contradict myself' (Walt Whitman) would be familiar to the bhakta. Laws of non-contradiction do not hold; successions of images may owe their logic to dream, trance, linguistic puzzle, the supernatural, the 'weird', etc.

3. A minimal art of maximum involvement. 'Intensity.' Meaning emerges in the poet's passion and fierce involvement in the art; hence romantic, not classical. The poem transfers its energy through conviction and the poet's personal white-hot experience of reality, not through rules of composition or delicate reworking of known themes. Honesty preferred to eloquence. The words and music may be rough, vernacular, and simple.

4. Listeners or spectators. These are public 'events'. The poet creates a theatre of participants, willing or unwilling. The poem implicates—pulls—the listener into its world. This 'world' is not a figure of speech; it is an alternative society, governed by love not law. Hectoring,

proselytizing, vows and oaths, fierce confrontation are not to make enemies but to draw the slothful or reluctant into relationship with the poet's alternative society. For similar reasons, there are warnings, pleas, curses, and outcries. Questions rather than answers. The poet actively constructs a counterculture, a community of visionaries who will live by the questions of the poem.

5. 'Animal-body-rootedness'. The poem is an act of both body and spirit. It calls attention to their inseparability: body-and-spirit; or to the complete ensheathment of one in the other. Dance, a potent 'technique of ecstasy', is frequently central to the performance, along with the full range of the vocal (growls, moans, sighs, and weeping). Sexuality can be channelled through the poem: a key element in raising the body to a state of vigilance or heightened sensitivity.

6. Poet as shaman. He or she is controller of the 'techniques of ecstasy'. The poet uses every available figure of language to reach insight or vision, and to make the vision available to a listener. Parallel to this: the poem is neither didactic nor descriptive. Its aim is to transfer the listener into other 'states'. The poem is not expository. It affects the participants and their landscape: time and space made sacred.

## Translation or 'Total Translation'

As a collection of India's bhakti poetry in English, this book is about translation as much as it is about the so-called original poems. I want to suggest—or provoke as a line of inquiry—that the original translation, the greatest shift the poem underwent, occurred long before it moved from Tamil or Bengali into English. It happened when some scribe wrote the poem down, lifting it from oral performance, setting it into a written script. With this act the poem was detached from the drum skin, the buzzing string of the *ektar* or tambura, the dancer's foot, or the community reciting its refrain back to the poet. It entered another realm (Robert Bringhurst: 'the solid form of language').

This means that '(u)nder the best circumstances translation-for-meaning is no more than partial translation', as Jerome Rothenberg wrote in the early 1970s. Poets and anthropologists—in the Americas, Europe, and Asia—collaborated for a time in the 1970s and 1980s on experiments they called 'total translation'. This was an effort to transfer 'words, sounds, (and to some extent) melody into a visual field'. Which meant attending to the presence of multiple voices, finding ways to locate distorted or 'meaningless' words in the new language that might meet the original, or fortuitously induce the same effect as the original (Eliade: 'to project the yogin'). The speaking or singing voice carries sounds that are not, strictly speaking, 'words'. In translation, these non-word elements are often the first items to vanish. So are polyphony, gesture, and ritual space.

I mention these efforts of a previous generation to emphasize that there are many ways to translate an oral work, many strata of intention and meaning to negotiate. And to suggest that the translators in this volume have had to take risks, meet with failure, and find satisfaction in strange places. If they have violated anyone's sense of what is proper, any specialist's lexical view of what is accurate, they have gone no farther than Antal or Tukaram did in their own day. Dennis Tedlock (1972) alerted translators to,

... the ongoing reopening of the ear and voice that Charles Olson called for all the way back in 1950, when he said that poetry must 'catch up and put into itself certain laws and possibilities of the breath.' The reopening of possibilities in our own language goes hand in hand, or voice in voice, with a new openness to the spoken words of other traditions ...

After the formal innovations in poetry during the past century, with the inclusion of many previously disregarded traditions—including the recognition of oral material as more than simply 'folklore'—readers can today see bhakti poetry, not as an argument within India's religious dialogue, but as a major contribution to world poetics.

## Nirguna or Saguna

The standard distinction, in scholarly and theological accounts of bhakti, take stock of whether the poet sings to a personalized deity that has not only a name but a definite form (*saguna*: with attributes, figurative); or whether the poet finds any description of spiritual reality to be a human limitation, a projection of personal fear, desire, expectation, rather than a true assertion about the personality of the universe (hence, *nirguna*: truth free of description, quality, attribute; non-figurative). The major saguna deities fall loosely into three forms: Vishnu, Siva, and particularly in the east, the goddess. In actuality, since bhakti often remains close to vernacular traditions, trying to disentangle any number of deities seems nearly fruitless. It is a task best left to the experts. In Bengal, Kali, Durga, and Uma readily shift into one another. In Maharashtra, a name for Vishnu may carry attributes identified elsewhere with Siva.

Some poets provide real dilemmas about where they fall in the nirguna–saguna distinction. Kabir is generally regarded as a pre-eminent nirguna figure. He speaks of Ram, but his is not the Ram of Tulsidas, nor of Valmiki, nor of any other epic or religious poet who conceives of a supernatural person or divinity. Kabir's Ram is a 'true name' (*Sat Nam*), a mystical experience not parsed through language. Kabir's poems of the *Bijak* point the way towards realization, they cannot describe it—as in Zen Buddhism the fatal error would be to mistake the finger pointing at the moon for the moon.

What can one say, then, of the western Kabir (translated in this volume by Ezra Pound), whose poems sound romantically Vaishnava, and assume the persona of a vigilant woman awaiting her lover? These are the poems the Sikhs preserve in their *Grantha* (scriptures), and the first to catch attention outside of India. Either we have two separate Kabirs (two separate 'Kabir traditions'), or a poet who, for various purposes, sang differently at different times.

Only a rigidly doctrinal approach to a poet such as Kabir would belittle his intelligence—reduce him sufficiently—to suggest that he could not move spontaneously (even humorously) between techniques, schools, movements (whatever we might call them), in his inquiries. In the end, I picture Kabir pinning us all with his walking dead-man's eye:

When death grips you by the hair,
where do your nirgun and sagun go?

## Received Tradition vs Historicity

Hardly a bhakti poet of note comes into the twenty-first century without a cloud of legend and uncertainty clinging to them. Their poetry (or song) is part of this cloud, and for many of them little attempt has ever been made to establish an authoritative edition of the work. For some poets—I have heard this said even of the renowned bhaktas Mirabai and Surdas—hardly a detail of the life can be authenticated, and it may be more accurate to speak of a 'tradition' known as, or signed by the name

Mirabai, than to claim historical certainty for an individual. The same goes for the authenticity of a poem.

What anyone attempting to survey bhakti poetry has to work with are the received traditions. These traditions are the outcome of historical, literary, and cultural forces: pressures, upheavals, fractures, eruptions. Not to speak of revisions. I expect scholars to wince at some choices I have made, or at certain translations I have included. Robert Bly's Kabir versions—done into American English, loosely, from the hopelessly stiff Victorian translations of Rabindranath Tagore and Evelyn Underhill— may sit far from any historical Kabir. The 'tradition' Tagore and Underhill worked with was itself based on hundreds of years of oral preservation, and collected into manuscript under circumstances far from modern text-critical methods. But as bhakti joins the international community of practising, contemporary poets, Bly's Kabir stands as deeply influential on what many outsiders regard as India's poetry. Likewise, a generation of North Americans, Japanese, and Europeans first heard of Ramprasad Sen through Gary Snyder:

## After Ramprasad Sen

Arms shielding my face
knees drawn up
Falling through flicker
Of womb after womb,
    through worlds,
Only begging, Mother,
    must I be born again?

Snyder says: you bear me, nurse me,
I meet you, always love you,
    you dance
    on my chest and thigh

Forever born again.

Allen Ginsberg's late bhakti compositions, 'After Lalon', which late in life he recited or sung to a *sruti* box he had purchased in India, were based on poems of the Baul, Lalon Shah (*ca.* 1774–1890?). To young westerners, Ginsberg's lyrics from the early 1990s were their first

exposure to the voice of the Baul. The fourth of Ginsberg's six poems
may sit closer to Lalon than Lalon did to his countryman Chandidas.

> Sleepless I stay up &
> think about my Death
> —certainly it's nearer
> than when I was ten
> years old
> and wondered how big the
> universe was—
> If I don't get some rest I'll die faster
> If I sleep I'll lose my
> chance for salvation—
> asleep or awake, Allen
> Ginsberg's in bed
> in the middle of the night.

## 'Bird Songs of an Old Man'

As an arrangement of India's bhakti poetry, this anthology is not more
than a beginning. I have tried to show the range of poems that occur
around the South Asian subcontinent, but have to recognize there exist
hundreds, even thousands of poets, whose work has not been translated
to English. It is possible many fine poets have never even had their work
written down. There are also religious definitions that need to be looked
at. Should Sufi, Buddhist, tribal or *adivasi*, and Sikh poets be included?
What about Jain, Christian, and non-affiliated creeds? Geographical
boundaries might be worth questioning too. What was going on in the
Himalayan kingdoms, or Sri Lanka, Bangladesh, or Burma?

I have a sense that literary approaches to bhakti have been secluded in
the domain of scholars and specialists, largely because the poems exist in
local dialects, and there is little reward for poets to do committed work
with the languages. A great deal more collaboration might be looked for
in the future, scholars and poets finding ways to move the work forward
in tandem—as in the present volume V. Narayana Rao has worked with
American poets.

My arrangement of this book has been to roughly sketch out the four
geographical compass points, and within that to keep poets together
within their particular languages. Future anthologies might find

it more useful to arrange the poets in other ways. I also think visual and sculptural modes—particularly the sort of non-iconic images Ajit Mukerjee has published in *Yoga Art* and other titles—would be worth bringing into discussion.

The great translators of South Asia—Marpa, Tulsidas, Vidyapati—and their counterparts in other parts of the world—Catullus, Chaucer, and Pound—have shown how poetry can be revitalized with discoveries drawn from other languages. These are poets who not only matched the excitement of the original poems but extended the range of poetry itself. Bhakti, with its dozens of languages and hundreds of vital poets, its rebellious spirit, erotic candour, and rough old use of the power of the spoken word, ought to draw more and more poets to its domain. As old assumptions about poetry (and of religion) get discarded as no longer useful, we can start to see many ways that bhakti brings poetics to a bedrock level of consciousness.

MAY 2011                                                    ANDREW SCHELLING

# SOUTH

# Early Tamil Poems to Siva

## Tipputtolar

The anthologies of classical Tamil poetry (*c.* 100 BCE–250 CE) hold
several poems to Murukan, 'the Red One', a war-god who at some later
point in history becomes identified with Siva. The following poem is an
archaic verse from the anthology *Kuruntokai*. It stands on the threshold
of bhakti, an early celebratory poem, a foretaste of things to come.

Red is the battlefield
as he crushes
the demons,

red his arrow shafts,

red the tusks
of his elephants:

this is the hill
of the Red One
with the whirling anklets,

the hill of red glory lilies,
flowers of blood.

—*Translated by A.K. Ramanujan*

# Nakkirar

The following poem, from Nakkirar's sixth-century *Tirumurukarruppatai*, or 'A Guide to Lord Murukan', is in the words of its translator A.K. Ramanujan, 'the earliest, long, full-fledged bhakti poem' in India. The section included here is the fifth of six parts, each devoted to a different aspect of Murukan. Ramanujan writes:

Murukan and his motifs appear in the earliest Tamil poems. He is a god of the mountain ... he is the Red One, god of love, war, and fertility. The poem pictures a whole community of men and women, with a god amid them, dancing, singing; the flowers and leaves they wear are emblematic of both erotic and warlike moods. When the poem ends, the chief dancer and the god he worships have become one ... Like certain shamans, a bhakta seeks to be a place, a vessel, for his chosen spirit who has chosen him.

The primal experience of bhakti that Ramanujan speaks of is one in which all the arts—melody, rhythm, dance, visualization, poetry—are 'techniques of ecstasy', a term coined by Mircea Eliade, referring to the arts of shamanism. In most cultures we know of, dance has been central to shamanic ritual, and one of the primordial methods for drawing down the attention of the gods. Ramanujan observes that the Tamil word for shaman is *camiyati*, 'god-dancer'. From Nakkirar to Mirabai, on through the Bengali Bauls, a lineage of bhakti emerges, in which dance remains at the centre of worship; it is good to keep in mind that the poem as we see it on the page is only a fraction of what was at its inception a much larger ritual or ceremony.

> The possessed shaman with the spear
> wears wreathes of green leaves
>     with aromatic nuts between them
> and beautiful long pepper,
>     wild jasmine and the three-lobed
>         white nightshade;
>
> his jungle tribes
>     have chests bright with sandal;
> the strong-bowed warriors

in their mountain village
drink with their kin
sweet liquor, honey brew
   aged in long bamboos
they dance rough dances
   hand in hand
      to the beat of small
         hillside drums;

the women
wear wreathes of buds
   fingered and forced to blossom
      so they smell differently,
wear garlands
   from the pools on the hill
      all woven into chains,
cannabis leaves
   in their dense hair,

white clusters
   from a sacred *katampu* tree
   red-trunked and flowering,
arrayed between large cool leaves
   for the male beetle to suck at,

in leaf skirts
   shaking
   on their jeweled mounds of venus,
and their gaits swaying with the innocence
   of peacocks;

the shaman
is the Red One himself,
is in red robes;

young leaf of the red-trunk *asoka*
flutters in his ears;

He wears a coat of mail
   a warrior band on his ankle,
      a wreath of scarlet ixora;

has a flute,
  a horn,
  several small instruments
  of music;

for vehicles
  he has a ram,
  a peacock;

a faultless rooster
  on his banner;

the Tall One
  with bracelets on his arms,
  with a bevy of girls, voices
    like lutestrings,
a cloth
cool-looking above the waist-band
tied so it hangs
all the way to the ground;

his hands large
  as drumheads
  hold gently
  several soft-shouldered
    fawn-like women;

he gives them proper places
  and he dances
  on the hills

and all such things happen
because
of His being
there.

And not only there.

—Translated by A.K. Ramanujan*

* Ramanujan, A.K. 1985. *Poems of Love and War, from the Eight Anthologies and the Ten Long Poems of Classical Tamil.* New York: Columbia University Press.

# Manikkavacakar

In the following poem, note not only the dance, but the way the poet performs his dance at the centre of his own poem: 'I bowed, I wept, danced, cried aloud, I sang, and I praised him.' The greatest noticeable shift from classical poems of the Tamil anthologies to the emergence of bhakti occurs in the stance of the poem's speaker. The anthology poems sound objective, descriptive, or they assume the voice of a dramatic character. The poet's own personality and experience lie far from the poem's centre. Ninth-century Saivite poet Manikkavacakar, by contrast, speaks from his own condition, a state of exaltation.

Not only does Manikkavacakar speak from the centre of the poem, but the poem is about his personal experience of the god's power. Here is the link back to the most archaic visionary state, well documented in pan-Asiatic shamanism and folklore—a state of intoxication with the divine. The poem also points forward to what lies at the heart of bhakti: an individual, unique relationship with the god. With this intense relationship comes a conviction about the uselessness of priests, a dismissal of clerical authority, organized religion, and social convention. Notice the visceral force of Manikka's imagery: 'Love pierced me / like a nail / driven into a green tree.' Then comes a declaration that will recur throughout bhakti, a refrain that in various forms will sound for a thousand years: 'I left shame behind.'

> He grabbed me
>     lest I go astray.
>
> Wax before an unspent fire,
>     mind melted,
>     body trembled.
>
> I bowed, I wept,
>     danced, and cried aloud,
>     I sang, and I praised him.
>
> Unyielding, as they say,
>     as an elephant's jaw

or a woman's grasp,
was love's unrelenting
seizure.

Love pierced me
    like a nail
        driven into a green tree.

Overflowing, I tossed
    like a sea,

heart growing tender,
body shivering,

while the world called me Demon!
and laughed at me,

I left shame behind,

took as an ornament
    the mockery of local folk.
Unswerving, I lost my cleverness
    in the bewilderment of ecstasy.

*—Translated by A.K. Ramanujan**

* Ramanujan, A.K. 1981. *Hymns for the Drowning: Poems for Visnu by Nammalvar.* Princeton, New Jersey: Princeton University Press.

# Alvar Poets

## Antal

'In the Tamil country of South India, between the sixth and the tenth centuries, there emerged a remarkable group of holy men and women who transformed the religious milieu of the south. Blazing a trail for the path of love, they emphasized utter surrender to a personal god ...' With these fairy-tale-like words, the translator and art critic Vidya Dehejia opens her account of Antal, the celebrated female poet of the Tamil tradition.

The poets of this earliest outbreak of bhakti in India can be divided into two groups: the Nayannars or Saivite singers, and the Alvars or Vaishnava singers. *Alvar* means 'one who has dived deep'—plunged into or drowned in Vishnu. There are twelve notable Alvars, and they form a pantheon of sorts. In the south their images in bronze and stone, or painted on walls, adorn numerous temples. They draw worshippers as fervently devoted to them as to the gods; stories full of marvels attach to them. Of the twelve Alvar poet-saints, only the one known as Antal, 'she who rules', is a woman.

The likeliest date for Antal is the first half of the ninth century, though scholars have inventively managed to place her as early as the eighth and late as the thirteenth century, based on an astronomical event in one poem:

Venus has risen
Jupiter has gone to slumber

The popular accounts of Antal's life come from two hagiographies: one Tamil, the other Sanskrit. The priest Visnucitta—himself an Alvar, known as Periyalvar—was hoeing the ground for his *tulsi* or holy basil, and discovered a baby girl embedded in the soil. He named her Kotai, 'Fragrant Braids', and raised her as if she were an incarnation of Bhudevi, 'Earth Goddess', a consort of Vishnu. As a child Kotai took to dressing up as a bride when her father was absent, and would wind in her hair the flower garland prepared for evening worship of Krishna. She admired herself at length before a glass, imagining herself Krishna's bride. Violating standards of purity, she would then return the garland to its place so it could be offered to the god. When her father finally caught her, he was horrified at the desecration, and withheld the garland from that evening's worship. During the night Vishnu appeared in a dream to Visnucitta, telling him the garland Kotai had worn was made fragrant and holy by her hair.

Antal dedicated herself to meditation on Vishnu, and began the two collections of poetry that come down to us with her name, the *Tiruppavai* and the *Nacciyar Tirumoli*. Her concerned father—unclear what to make of his daughter's fixation on Krishna, and her stubborn refusal to wed a human husband—learnt from a later dream that Vishnu intended to marry her. A wedding was organized at great expense, and Antal was carried to Vishnu's temple at Rankanata in a bridal procession. When the retinue arrived, Antal climbed from the palanquin. She approached the image of Vishnu, embraced its feet, climbed onto the serpent couch, and vanished. This absorption of her physical body into her god is the first instance in the annals of bhakti, a disappearance that shows up in lore of many women bhakti poets. Mirabai, Muktabai, and Lal Ded will all be similarly absorbed.

The following verses come from the fourteen cantos of Antal's *Nacciyar Tirumoli*, or 'Anguish of Separation'. They draw heavily on conventions of classical Tamil. They depend equally on stories of Krishna, and are full of pan-Indian themes from love poetry: the prevalence of Kamadeva; the dispatch of a bird-messenger to the beloved; the grove of Krishna's love affairs; the erotic promise of impending rain clouds; the agony of separation.

O ancient one,
I wrote your name
upon the wall.
For you I drew the sugarcane bow,
banner with emblem of fish,
attendant maidens,
retinue of horses.
From early childhood
I yearned for
the lord of Dvarka,
adored him alone,
dedicated to him
my budding breasts.
Kamadeva, unite me to him soon.                                    (1.4)

I dedicated my swelling breasts
to the lord who holds
the conch and flaming discus.
If there is even a whisper
of giving me to a mortal,
I shall not live.
O Manmatha,
would you permit a roving jackal
to sniff and eat
the sacrificial food
the Brahmins offer
to celestial gods?                                                  (1.5)

To keep my vow
I eat but once a day,
body neglected, unadorned,
tangled hair in disarray,
lips pale and dry.
O Kamadeva of eternal glory

for one thing I plead with you,
fulfill my womanhood!
Let glory be mine
that I held the feet of Kesava.                    (1.7)

Learned Brahmins
chanted Vedic mantras,
placed green *dharba* grass
around the sacrificial fire
lit with twigs.
The lord of great prowess,
strong as a raging elephant,
took my hand,
we walked around the fire—
I dreamt this dream, my friend.              (6.7)

O clouds
from whose body
lightning springs,
tell the lord of Venkata
upon whose glorious body
rests the goddess Sri,
that I yearn incessantly
that he should desire
the budding breasts
of my radiant body—that he should come
and fold me in embrace.                       (8.4)

O great rain clouds
that rend the sky,
let your heavy showers
make the honeyed blossoms of Venkata
fall and scatter.
Go to the lord who killed Hiranya,
rent him open
with his sharp claws—
tell him to return
the bracelets
he took from me.                              (8.5)

O cool clouds
that rise into the skies
laden with water,
spread yourselves,
let your showers
fall upon Venkata,
the hill of the lord
who took the earth from Mahabali.
The gnat
entering the woodpile
hollows it—
the lord entering me
has taken all
consumed my womanhood.
O great rain clouds
tell Narana
of my grievous
love-sickness.                                                   (8.6)

They will behold
the face of none but
the lord who holds the discus
in his lustrous palm.
These breasts of mine
clad in red *choli*
close their eyes,
draw back from shame
from mere mortals.
They will not go
to any but Govinda.
No longer can I live here—
take me please
to the banks of the Yamuna.                          (12.4)

'Govinda! Govinda!'
my parrot calls from its cage.
If I scold it, refuse it food,
it calls out loudly

'O lord who measured the worlds!'
Friends, do not lose your fair name
do not earn dishonor.
Send me soon
to that city of stately mansions—take me to Dvarka.          (12.9)

I hunger and thirst
for a sight
of Kannan, my dark lord.
Don't stand aside
mocking me—
your words sting
like sour juice
poured upon an open wound.
Go bring the yellow silk
wrapped around the waist
of him who knows not
the sorrow of women—
fan me with it,
cool the burning of my heart.          (13.1)

I am caught in the snare
of that omniscient lord
who slumbered
upon the banyan leaf.
Do not speak
whatever comes to mind—
your words pierce me
like a dagger.
The cowherd chief
who tends his calves
with staff in hand,
that dancer with the waterpots
who reclines in sacred Kutanai—
bring me
his sacred basil
cool, lustrous, blue,

place it
upon my soft tresses.                                        (13.2)

Like an arrow
from the bow of his eyebrows,
the sidelong glance
of him who destroyed Kamsa
enters my heart,
makes me sore with pain,
weak and worn.
I yearn, I melt,
yet he says not
'have no fear'.
If willingly
he gives his garland
of holy basil,
bring it,
place it upon my breast.                                     (13.3)

He who flies
the victory banner of Garuda,
whom all the worlds exalt,
his mother reared him
like the bitter margosa tree
to serve no purpose.
To wipe away the sorrow
of these innocent breasts,
the sorrow of not finding him,
hold them tight
against his youthful shoulders,
bind them there.                                             (13.7)

My soul melts in anguish—
he cares not
if I live or die.
If I see the lord of Govardhana
that looting thief,

that plunderer,
I shall pluck
by their roots
these useless breasts,
I shall fling them
at his chest,
I shall cool
the raging fire
within me.                                                    (13.8)


To soothe the grief
of my rounded breasts,
is it not better
in this very birth
to serve Govinda
in little intimate ways,
than wait for a life beyond?
If one day
he would fold me
into his radiant chest,
that would fulfill me.
Else, looking straight at me,
uttering the truth,
he should give me
leave to go—
that also I would accept.                                     (13.9)


Kotai of Visnucittan
master of the town of Villiputuvai,
she of excellence
whose eyebrows arch like a bow,
poured out her intense longing for
the radiant light of Ayarpati
the lord who brought her pain.
Those who chant
these verses of praise

will never flounder
in the sea of sorrow.                                           (13.10)
                                        —*Translated by Vidya Dehejia**

# Nammalvar

Of the twelve Alvar poets who composed in Tamil and lived between the sixth and ninth centuries, Nammalvar is considered the greatest. Known by a variety of names, including Maran and Catakopan, to most people he holds the affectionate title Nammalvar, 'our own Alvar'. Historians propose 880 and 930 CE as his dates. As with many bhakti poets, the facts of his life are vague, but the legends vivid.

When Nammalvar was born—in Tirukurukur, Tamil Nadu, of peasant caste—his mother offered her breast but the infant ignored it. He seemed mute and deaf, never whimpered or cried, and lay where his parents placed him, motionless. Confounded and troubled, his parents took the child to a local Vishnu statue and left him at its feet. The boy rose to a standing position—the first gesture of his own volition—strode to a huge tamarind tree, climbed into a hollow in its trunk, and took the seated posture of a yogin, his eyes closed.

At that time a wandering poet in north India, Maturakavi, was on the bank of the Ganges. In the southern sky a bright star flared. For three days the poet followed the star, and was led to Kurukur where he found the child seated inside the tamarind trunk. Maturakavi tried to rouse the boy, shouting, gesturing, and knocking stones against a nearby temple wall. The boy did not move. Finally the pilgrim approached the hollow in the tree and asked:

'Master, if the spirit is sheathed in matter, what does it eat? Where does it rest?'
'*That* it will eat, and *there* it rests,' was the instant reply.

* Dehejia, Vidya. 1990. *Antal and Her Path of Love: Poems of a Woman Saint from South India*. Albany, New York: State University of New York Press.

The spirit feeds on *that*, the holy; it dwells *there*, in the holy. With this declaration the boy yogin broke his muteness and sang out the 1,102 verses of the *Tiruvaymoli*, or 'Holy Word of Mouth'. This set of poems—spontaneously projected rather than laboured over—came to be called 'the ocean of the Tamil Veda, in which the Upanisads of the thousand branches flow together'. It comprises a single continuous song, each hymn linked to the previous by opening with the final word of the hymn that went before. Because of this formal linkage, and the circular sense of the poem it provides, A.K. Ramanujan calls *Tiruvaymoli*, 'an icon for the endless, ever-changing forms of the Lord'.

Notice also the unorthodox method of composition. The child saint had studied no grammars or textbooks of verse, immersed himself in no scripture, sat by no guru. At the moment of ripening, his songs erupt, complete, interlinked in complex ways, and unrevised.

Nammalvar's songs—sung forth without forethought or revision—come grouped into tens, the tens into hundreds, and finally into a thousand. These numbers are more symbolic than actual, as each gathering includes a *phalasruti* verse, or 'recital of the fruits', an account of the merit derived by singing it. Individual verses stand alone as poems, and get recited or quoted as if they stand independently. Ramanujan, the translator of Nammalvar, calls them 'forebears of later traditions of Vaisnava poetry ... Characteristic pan-Indian themes find some of their first and finest expression in the poetry of the alvars.' Among these themes: the god's *lila* or divine play which lies at the root of both misery and delight; Krishna's mischievous childhood and erotic adolescence; the relationship of singer to god as two lovers. Dramatic voices appear, in particular the singer as a girl longing for her beloved or devastated by his infidelity. Note too the Vaishnavite iconography: conch shell, wheel, yellow robes, basil.

Bhakti evolves a new type of devotee, far closer to the archaic shaman than to a priest or pious citizen. For Nammalvar, the poet is in constant relationship with the god, at times even possessed by him. This inner conviction allows him to spurn good manners and social customs, ignore the customary training of the poet, flout religious authority, and insist that anyone—of any caste, gender, or occupation—can be a singer for the Lord.

O lord unending
    wearing honey flowers
        and basil leaf
    in your hair

tell us this:

as moon
    as sun
        as the amazing numberless stars

as darkness
    and as torrents of rain

as honor
    as shame

and as death
    with his cruel eyes

how fantastic
    can you get?


## What She Said

Evening has come,
    but not the Dark one.

The bulls,
    their bells ringing
        have mated with the cows
and the cows are frisky.

The flutes play cruel songs,
    bees flutter in their bright
    white jasmine
    and the blue lily.

The sea leaps into the sky
    and cries aloud.

Without him here,
   what shall I say?
   how shall I survive?

## What She Said

Our Kannan dark as rain cloud
   has stolen my heart
   and it has gone away with him
     all by itself.

But this north wind
   seems ready for battle.

Gathering the sweet smoke of incense,
   the beauty of lutestrings,
   the fifth tune of night and love,
   and cool moist sandal

it blows and blows,
   culling on its way
   the fragrance of new jasmine,

and it burns;

how can I say anything to anyone
O mother?

## What Her Mother Said

O women,
   you too have daughters
   and have brought them up.

How can I tell you
   about my poor girl?

She talks of the conch shell,
   she talks of the wheel,

and she talks, night and day,
of the basil in his hair,

what shall I do?

## What Her Mother Said

When she sees kings,
she says, I see my lord.

When she sees shapes and colors,
she leaps up, saying,
I see him who measured the world.

All temples with gods in their wombs
are, she says, places of the lord dark as the sea.

In terror, in love, in every mood,
she wants
the Dark One's anklet's.

For the sake of that girl,
her mouth red as a berry,
you broke the seven bulls;

you bent the long bow
and finished off the king
of the island of towers;

and you broke the tusk
of that pedigreed elephant.

I haven't worshipped you
with flowers and holy water
at proper times;

but then
my heart is the only sandalwood
to rub and perfume your body with,

your body
   dark as *kaya* blossom.

You roam the seas
   the mountains, the skies,
you touch them lightly,

cold north wind!

Night and day,
   lit by alternate lamps
      of sun and moon,
like us
you wander sleepless:

are you also craving,
since the time
   time began,

for a glimpse
   of our lord of the mighty wheel?

Kings
   who rule the whole earth all alone
   for long years

will one day hobble
on legs bitten by black dogs

and beg from a broken pot
here
   in this very life
with the whole world watching

don't tarry then

think of the lord's feet
and live

## What She Said

Making the earth shiver,
    crowding and wetting the world
        with their waters,
scratching with their hooves,

the dark blue bulls of heaven
fight with each other.

And I,
    doing good and evil,
cannot tell what's before me:

    is it or is it not
    the cold monsoon
    bearing the shape
    of my dark lord,

speaking of his cruelty,
        his going away?


## What He Said

The sight I see now
is rare indeed.

Even as I say, 'Dear girl,
    dear as our Dark One's paradise,
I've got to go away and far away
to get rich,'

her eyes
bring enough to buy a world,

eyes,
    each large as the palm of a hand,
    shaped like a carp,
dropping pearls
and grief yellow as gold.

## What She Said

Skin dark as young mango leaf
   is wilting
Yellow patches spread all over me.
Night is as long as several lives.

All these are the singular dowry
my good heart brings
as she goes over

   to the cool basil
   of my lord, the Dark One
with the wheel that cuts down demons.

## What She Said to Her Girlfriend

Dear friend,
   dear as the Dark One's paradise,

night grows long, many lives long,
   when we part;
or goes fast, a split second many times split,
   when we are together.

So I suffer even when my lover joins me
   many nights in a row,
and suffer again
   when he goes away.

Blessed night, ever flowing,
   is full of tricks,
   plays fast and loose.

## What Her Foster Mother Said

She's young:
   breasts not even full grown;
   hair thick, soft, but much too short;

her dress doesn't cover her waist
and her tongue stammers;

but her eyes,
    so priceless
    earth and sea cannot buy them,
    they flash everywhere.

She's learning to say,
    'Is Venkatam
    the hill of our Lord?'

Will she ever get there?

## What Her Girlfriend Said

They haven't flowered yet,
the fat *konrai* trees,
nor hung out their garlands
    and golden circlets
in their sensual canopy of leaves
along the branches,

dear girl,
dear as the paradise of our lord
who measured the earth
    girdled by the restless sea,

they are waiting
with buds
for the return
of your lover
    once twined in your arms.


My girl, who's just learning to speak
says,
    'I'm beyond all learning.
    I'm all the learning you learn.'

'I'm the cause of all learning,
   I end all learning,
I'm the essence of all learning,'
        says she.

Does my girl talk this way
   because our lord of all learning
      has come and taken her over?

How can I tell you,
   O learned men!

My lord
   who swept me away forever
      into joy that day,

made me over into himself

and sang in Tamil
his own songs
through me:

what shall I say
   to the first of things,
      flame
         standing there,

what shall I say
   to stop?

Being all three worlds
   and nothing

being desire
   being rage
being both the flower-born Laksmi
   and anti-Laksmi
      black goddess of ill-luck

being both honor and shame

our lord
   lives in Vinnakar
      city named Sky
which the gods worship lovingly

and in my evil heart
he lives forever
   flame of flames.

*—Translated by A.K. Ramanujan*[*]

* Ramanujan, A.K., 1981. *Hymns for the Drowning: Poems for Visnu by Nammalvar*. Princeton, New Jersey: Princeton University Press.

# Virasaiva Poets

## Devara Dasimayya

Beginning in the tenth century a group of poets, the Virasaivas or 'Heroes of Siva', began to appear in the Tamil speaking regions. Devara Dasimayya is the earliest on record. He was born in the tenth century in Mudanaru, a village renowned for its many temples. Among these temples is one dedicated to Ramanatha (Lord of Rama), the manifestation of Siva said to have been worshipped by Rama. Each of Dasimayya's *vacana*s, or songs, invokes or, more accurately, addresses Ramanatha. As with all the Virasaiva poets, the name of the poet's personal deity serves as the poet's signature.

Legends and miracles surround Dasimayya, who spent time as a homeless mendicant, then worked as a weaver after Siva appeared and told him that asceticism was a less effective method of devotion than work in the world. The cycles of story refer to conversions Dasimayya made among local tribal groups, turning them from centuries-old blood sacrifice to a peaceful devotion to Siva. He is also credited with converting Jains, and debating with and often converting orthodox brahmins. Several of his poems disputing any essential difference between men and women sound almost postmodern, though in their own day they would have cut at the assertions of orthodoxy.

Without doubt Dasimayya was an active proselytizer, setting the course for a strong Saivite period in the south. A.K. Ramanujan, his translator into English, notes that the legends point to the tenth century as a period of fierce conflict between Virasaiva devotees and competing traditions.

In the mother's womb
the child does not know
his mother's face

nor can *she* ever know
his face.

The man in the world's illusion
does not know the Lord

nor the Lord him,

Ramanatha.


A fire
in every act and look and word.
Between man and wife
a fire.
In the plate of food
eaten after much waiting
a fire.
In the loss of gain
a fire.
And in the infatuation
of coupling
a fire.

You have given us
five fires
and poured dirt in our mouths

O Ramanatha.


A man filled grain
in a tattered sack

and walked all night
fearing the toll-gates

but the grain went through the tatter
and all he got was a gunny sack.

It is thus
with the devotion
of the faint-hearted

O Ramanatha.


When a man is of the Lord
and his wife, of the world,
what they eat is still
shared equally:

it is like
bringing a dead dog
into the attic
and sharing bits
of its carcass,

O Ramanatha.


You have forged
this chain
of eighteen links
and chained us humans:

you have ruined us
O Ramanatha
and made us dogs forever
on the leash.


Did the breath of the mistress
have breasts and long hair?

Or did the master's breath
wear sacred thread?

Did the outcaste, last in line,
hold with his outgoing breath
the stick of his tribe?

What do the fools of the world know
of the snares you set,
O Ramanatha?


To the utterly at-one with Siva

there's no dawn,
no new moon,
no noonday,
nor equinoxes,
nor sunsets,
nor full moons;

his front yard
is the true Benares,

O Ramanatha.


If they see
breasts and long hair coming
they call it woman,

if beard and whiskers
they call it man:

but, look, the self that hovers
in between
is neither man
nor woman

O Ramanatha.


Suppose you cut a tall bamboo
in two;
make the bottom piece a woman,

the headpiece a man;
rub them together
till they kindle:
    tell me now,
the fire that's born,
is it male or female,

    O Ramanatha?

                                    —*Translated by A.K. Ramanujan**

# Allama Prabhu

Allama is survived by something over 1,300 vacanas or songs. He probably lived in the eleventh, possibly the twelfth century, slightly earlier than the other renowned Virasaiva poets. His title is *Prabhu*, master, and if the stories are true, he served as a living exemplar, or even a goad to Basavanna and Mahadeviyakka. Most of his songs carry the name Guhesvara, Lord of Caves, and hold the strangest and most paradoxical imagery in the Virasaiva tradition.

If mountains shiver in the cold
with what
will they wrap them?

If space goes naked
with what
shall they clothe it?

The use of cryptic, esoteric symbols, illogic, ambiguity, and riddle, is old in India's tradition. The Sanskrit term *sandhyabhasa*, 'twilight speech', or perhaps 'intentional speech', refers to a tradition of cryptography in place since Vedic times. Masters of yoga and tantra employed it to conceal secret teachings from the uninitiated. In the Tamil tradition, lyrics that use occult imagery and illogical paradox are termed *bedgaina vacana*, or fancy poems. One of their effects is to crack the listener's

---

* Ramanujan, A.K. 1973. *Speaking of Siva*. Baltimore; Penguin Books.

mind open, jolting it from domestic convention or common logic. These poems do not describe an experience of spiritual freedom, their intent is to provoke it. In this way they stand close to mantra or spell, actively recovering one of poetry's archaic mandates: to contact the supernatural, the divine, or the powers hidden within. Allama employed this sort of mind-cracking riddle, along with 'mockery, invective, argument, poetry, loving kindness and sheer presence', according to A.K. Ramanujan, and his effectiveness is honoured in the title Prabhu.

He lived in Kalyana, and it was his reputation as well as Basavanna's evangelizing that made that city a center of the Virasaiva bhaktas. Evidently his charismatic presence drew a constant line of seekers to Kalyana. These pilgrims called the community they founded *Anubhava*, 'halls of experience'.

The fifteenth-century poet Harihara recounts one of the vivid legends. Allama is the son of a temple dance instructor, and is himself a temple drummer. He falls in love with Kamalate, 'Love's Tendril', marries her, and the two become absorbed in their lovemaking, without beginning, middle, or end. But a fever sweeps through the district and Kamalate succumbs to it. Allama, inconsolable, stumbles about in grief. He staggers across the countryside calling for Kamalate. Sitting in a grove, scraping the ground with his foot, he uncovers the pinnacle of a temple buried in the earth, like 'the nipple on the breast of Goddess Freedom'. Allama digs down to its portal which he kicks in and enters. Seated within is a yogin, absorbed in concentration on a linga. Long dreadlocks, a necklace of rudrakshi beads, serpent earrings, his eyes unblinking—his name Animisayya, Open Eyes. As Allama stares, Animisayya makes over to him a linga; then the yogin's life drains away. It has been a moment of magically preordained transmission, occurring in a wordless realm, and Allama is enlightened.

Very likely it is this temple long buried in an underground grotto that Allama invokes in the name Guhesvara, Lord of Caves. Also worth noting: the transmission by a guru. In the annals of bhakti, the figure of the guru rises to importance, often of greater interest than that of the deity.

It's dark above the clutching hand.
It's dark over the seeing eye.

It's dark over the remembering heart.
It's dark here
   with the Lord of Caves
   out there.


A wilderness grew
in the sky.
In that wilderness
a hunter.
In the hunter's hands
a deer.

   The hunter will not die
   till the beast
   is killed.

Awareness is not easy,
is it,
O Lord of Caves?


The fire of the city burned in the forest,
forest fires burned in the town.
Listen, listen to the flames
of the four directions.
Flapping and crackling in the vision
a thousand bodies dance in it
and die countless deaths,

O Lord of Caves.


Poets of the past
are the children of my concubines.
Poets to come
are infants of my pity.
The poets of the sky
are babies in my cradle.

Visnu and Brahma
are my kinsmen and sidekicks.

You are the father-in-law
and I the son-in-law,

O Lord of Caves.


One dies,
another bears him to the burial ground:
still another takes them both
and burns them.

No one knows the groom
and no one knows the bride.
Death falls across
the wedding.

Much before the decorations fade
the bridegroom is dead.

Lord, only your men
have no death.


In the mortar without water,
pestles without shadows.

Women without bodies
pound rice without grains,

and sing lullabies
to the barren woman's son.

Under the streamers of fire,
plays the child of the Lord.


Some say
they saw It.
What is It,

the circular sun,
the circle of the stars?

The Lord of the Caves
lives in the town
of the moon mountain.


For all their search
   they cannot see
   the image in the mirror.

It blazes in the circles
   between the eyebrows.
   Who knows this
   has the Lord.


Feed the poor
tell the truth
make water-places
for the thirsty
and build tanks for a town—

   you may then go to heaven
   after death, but you'll get nowhere
   near the truth of Our Lord.

And the man who knows Our Lord,
he gets no results.


Looking for your light,
I went out:

   it was like the sudden dawn
   of a million million suns,

   a ganglion of lightnings
   for my wonder.

O Lord of Caves,
if you are light,
there can be no metaphor.

*—Translated by A.K. Ramanujan**

# Basavanna

Of the renowned Virasaiva poets, Basavanna had the greatest public exposure. Many accounts of his life come down to us, full of contradictions. He is a saint, a ruthlessly honest poet, and the visionary founder of a community of Virasaivas to his followers. To Jains and Buddhists, who were vying for political influence at the time and had seen their power sapped in the wake of Basavanna's reforms, he is a demonic, conspiratorial figure. He was a burr in the side of orthodox brahmins, drawing the faithful away to his egalitarian kingdom free of caste or gender bias.

Born in 1106, devoted to Siva from a young age, he found the caste system repugnant, his brahmin upbringing a constriction, and orthodox ritual absurd. 'Love of Siva cannot live with ritual,' wrote Harihara 400 years later, describing how Basavanna cast off his family, social propriety, material wealth, and travelled to Kudalasanga, Place of Joining Rivers. Here he found his personal form of Siva, Kudalasangadeva, Lord of the Meeting Rivers, who visited him in dreams. At his god's urging he moved to Kalyana, where through family contacts he became courtier and eventually a close friend to King Bijjala. With the king's approval Basavanna sent out a call for Siva devotees, drawing them from afar, initiating novices, aggressively recruiting, and finally transforming the region into a new kingdom or community of bhaktas.

This bhakta community not only rejected caste, class, and gender inequalities, but substituted for familiar ceremonies a set of symbolic items, including a linga worn by every member. Their only mantra, the five-syllabic (*pancaksara*) prayer '*nama-Sivaya*' they referred to as

* Ramanujan, A.K. 1973. *Speaking of Siva*. Baltimore; Penguin Books.

'weightier than the 70 million other mantras put together'. But the new community gathered enemies. Intriguers made their case to Bijjala, and the parents of a mixed-caste Virasaiva couple were dragged to death 'in the dust and the thorn of the streets', (Ramanujan). Riots erupted, rampaging Virasaivas stabbed King Bijjala to death, and Basavanna, who had tried to quell the violence, returned to his place of meeting rivers. He died shortly after, in about 1168.

Futile as a ghost,
I stand guard over hidden gold

O lord of the meeting rivers.


The rich
will make temples for Siva.
What shall I,
a poor man,
do?

My legs are pillars,
the body the shrine,
the head a cupola
of gold.

Listen, O lord of the meeting rivers,
things standing shall fall,
but the moving ever shall stay.


The master of the house, is he at home, or isn't he?
    Grass on the threshold,
    dirt in the house:
The master of the house, is he at home, or isn't he?

    Lies in the body,
    lust in the heart:
no, the master of the house is not at home,
    our Lord of the Meeting Rivers.

When a whore with a child
takes on a customer for money,

neither child not lecher
will get enough of her.

She'll go pat the child once,
then go lie with the man once,

neither here nor there.
Love of money is relentless,

my lord of the meeting rivers.


A snake-charmer and his noseless wife,
snake in hand, walk carefully
trying to read the omens
for a son's wedding,

but they meet head-on
a noseless woman
and her snake-charming husband,
and cry, 'The omens are bad!'

His own wife has no nose;
there's a snake in his hand.
What shall I call such fools
who do not know themselves

and see only the others,

     O Lord
     of the meeting
     rivers!


The sacrificial lamb brought for the festival
ate up the green leaf brought for the decorations.

Not knowing a thing about the kill,
it wants only to fill its belly:
born that day, to die that day.

But tell me:
   did the killers survive,
   O lord of the meeting rivers?


Before
   the grey reaches the cheek,
   the wrinkle the rounded chin
   and the body becomes a cage of bones:

before
   with fallen teeth
   and bent back
   you are someone else's ward:

before
   you drop your hand to the knee
   and clutch a staff:

before
   age corrodes
   your form:

before
   death touches you:

   worship
   our lord
   of the meeting rivers!


I don't know anything like time-beats and metre
nor the arithmetic of strings and drums;
I don't know the count of iamb and dactyl.

My lord of the meeting rivers,
as nothing will hurt you
I'll sing as I love.

The pot is a god. The winnowing
fan is a god. The stone in the
street is a god. The comb is a
god. The bowstring is also a
god. The bushel is a god and the
spouted cup is a god.

Gods, gods, there are so many
there's no place left
for a foot.

   There is only
one god. He is our Lord
of the Meeting Rivers.


Look here, dear fellow:
I wear these clothes
only for you.

Sometimes I am man,
sometimes I am woman.

O lord of the meeting rivers
I'll make wars for you
but I'll be your devotees' bride.


When
like a hailstone crystal
like a waxwork image
the flesh melts in pleasure
   how can I tell you?

The waters of joy
broke the banks
and ran out of my eyes.

I touched and joined
my lord of the meeting rivers.

How can I talk to anyone
of that?

—Translated by A.K. Ramanujan*

# Mahadeviyakka

Of the Virasaiva poets, Mahadeviyakka has stood out for centuries as the most vivid figure. She was born in Udutadi village, in Sivamogga, but considered as her true birth an initiation into the mysteries of Siva by an unknown guru at age ten. The local temple had an image of Siva as Mallikarjuna, the Jasmine White One, to which Mahadevi added the term Cenna, Lovely. Each of her vacanas carries *Cennamallikarjuna*, Lord Lovely White Jasmine, as its *ankita*, or signature.

Like Antal before her, and Mirabai after, she considered herself betrothed to her Lord and refused human lovers. She must have been quite beautiful. The stories tell of many men who tried to win her, though finally a local chieftain, Kausika, managed to marry her. Many of her songs play on the conflict between her Lord white as jasmine and her mortal husband.

> Mother,
> because they all have thorns
> in their chests,
>     I cannot take
> any man in my arms but my lord
>     white as jasmine.

At some point she deserted her husband, her family, her social ties, and took to wandering. In an act of supreme defiance she abandoned her clothes, wearing only long tresses to cover herself. She found her way to Kalyana, where Allama and Basavanna had gathered many followers into the Halls of Experience.

---

* Ramanujan, A.K. 1973. *Speaking of Siva*. Baltimore; Penguin Books.

Allama received her, and their conversation—between sceptical guru and wildly devotional student—is central to Virasaivite lore. Many of Mahadeviyakka's songs are said to have emerged from these dialogues. When Allama asked to whom she was married, she replied, 'the White Jasmine Lord.' Allama then inquired why she would travel unclad, as though she could leave delusion behind with her clothes. Furthermore, if she is so liberated from convention, why does she cover herself with her hair? Her reply—

> Till the fruit is ripe inside
> the skin will not fall off.
> I'd a feeling it would hurt you
> if I displayed the body's seals of love.
> O brother, don't tease me
> needlessly. I'm given entire
> into the hands of my lord
> white as jasmine.
> (Ramanujan's translation)

Her defiance and youthful bravery lend her a vivid shawl of legend. A.K. Ramanujan refers to her as a 'love-child'. She must have looked similar to the flower children of the early 1970s, who swarmed college campuses worldwide, at the time he was preparing his translations in Chicago. Yet this depiction of her, as an unrealistic or dreamy figure, stands at odds with the force of her poetry. Her fellow Virasaiva poets considered her the finest, the most deeply realized of them all, and her vacanas are neither rough nor unlearned. They follow the precise moods of love explored in Sanskrit poetry. Reworking the traditional phases, she depicts herself as the heroine in the three poignant contexts: illicit love with a secret paramour, anguished lover separated from her beloved, and rapturous girl tasting the pleasures of sexual union. 'In her,' says Ramanujan, 'the phases of human love are metaphors for the phases of mystic ascent.' Like Mirabai several centuries later, she insists she has come 'through eighty-four hundred thousand vaginas', born lifetime after lifetime to pursue her beloved.

> Like a silkworm weaving
> her house with love
> from her marrow,

and dying
in her body's threads
winding tight, round
and round
   I burn
desiring what the heart desires.

Cut through, O lord,
my heart's greed,
and show me
your way out,

O lord white as jasmine.


Not one, not two, not three or four,
but through eighty-four thousand vaginas
have I come,
   I have come
through unlikely worlds,
      guzzled on
pleasure and pain.
      Whatever be
all previous lives,
   show me mercy
this one day,
   O lord
   white as jasmine.


Locks of shining red hair
a crown of diamonds
small beautiful teeth
and eyes in a laughing face
that light up fourteen worlds—
   I saw his glory
and seeing, I quell today
the famine in my eyes.

I saw the haughty Master
for whom men, all men
are but women, wives.

I saw the Great One
who plays at love
with Sakti,
original to the world,

I saw His stance
and began to live.


Would a circling surface vulture
    know such depths of sky
    as the moon would know?

would a weed on the riverbank
    know such depths of water
    as the lotus would know?

would a fly darting nearby
    know the smell of flowers
    as the bee would know?

O lord white as jasmine
    only you would know
    the way of your devotees:
    how would these,

these
    mosquitoes
    on the buffalo's hide?


Listen, sister, listen.
I had a dream.

I saw rice, betel, palmleaf
and coconut.

I saw an ascetic
come to beg,
white teeth and small matted curls.

I followed on his heels
and held his hand,
he who goes breaking
all bounds and beyond.

I saw the lord, white as jasmine,
and woke wide open.

He bartered my heart,
    looted my flesh,
    claimed as tribute
    my pleasure,
    took over
    all of me.

I'm the woman of love
for my lord, white as jasmine.

Other men are thorn
under the smooth leaf.
I cannot touch them,
go near them, nor trust them,
nor speak to them confidences.

Mother,
because they all have thorns
in their chests,
        I cannot take
any man in my arms but my lord

    white as jasmine.

Husband inside,
lover outside.
I can't manage them both.

This world
and that other,
cannot manage them both.

O lord white as jasmine

I cannot hold in one hand
both the round nut
and the long bow.


Who cares
      who strips a tree of leaf
      once the fruit is plucked?

Who cares
      who lies with a woman
      you have left?

Who cares
      who ploughs the land
      you have abandoned?

After this body has known my lord
      who cares if it feeds
      a dog
      or soaks up water?


People,
male and female,
blush when a cloth covering their shame
comes loose.
      When the lord of lives
lives drowned without a face
in the world, how can you be modest?

When all the world is the eye of the lord,
onlooking everywhere, what can you
cover and conceal?

Make me go from house to house
   with arms stretched for alms.
If I beg, make them give nothing.
If they give, make it fall to the ground.
If it falls, before I pick it up, make a dog take it,
O lord
white as jasmine.


I love the Handsome One:
   he has no death
   decay nor form
   no place or side
   no end or birthmarks.
   I love him O mother. Listen.

I love the Beautiful One
   with no bond nor fear
   no clan no land
   no landmarks
   for his beauty.

So my lord, white as jasmine, is my husband.

Take these husbands who die,
   decay, and feed them
   to your kitchen fire!


O brothers, why do you talk
   to this woman,
   hair loose,
   face withered,
   body shrunk?

O fathers, why do you bother
   with this woman?
   She has no strength of limb,
   has lost the world,

    lost power of will,
    turned devotee,

she has lain down
with the Lord, white as jasmine,
and has lost caste.


Riding the blue sapphire mountains
wearing moonstone for slippers
blowing long horns
O Siva
when shall I
crush you on my pitcher breasts

O lord white as jasmine
when do I join you
stripped of body's shame
and heart's modesty?


If He says
He has to go away
to fight battles at the front
   I understand and can be quiet.

But how can I bear it
when He is here in my hands
right here in my heart
   and will not take me?

O mind, O memory of pasts,
if you will not help me get to Him
how can I ever bear it?


I look at the road
for his coming.
If he isn't coming,
I pine and waste away.

If he is late,
I grow lean.

O mother, if he is away
for a night,
I'm like the lovebird (*cakravaka*)
with nothing
in her embrace.


Better than meeting
and mating all the time
is the pleasure of mating once
after being far apart.

When he's away
I cannot wait
to get a glimpse of him.

Friends, when will I have it
both ways,
be with Him
yet not with Him,
my lord white as jasmine?

*—Translated by A.K. Ramanujan*[*]

# Sule Sankavva

Sankavva is represented by only a single surviving poem. It is in the Kannada language, and comes from the twelfth century, making her a contemporary of Mahadeviyakka. The ankita or name of Siva to whom she sings is *Nirlajjeshvara*—'the god without shame'. *Ishvara* could also be translated as Siva.

* Ramanujan, A.K. 1973. *Speaking of Siva*. Baltimore: Penguin Books.

In the first line she speaks of herself as a prostitute. Susie Tharu and K. Lalita (1993) write, 'Although many of the poet-saints of the bhakti movement were artisans and people who plied small trades, it is unusual to find one who was a prostitute.' There is too little here, though—a single brief poem—to be certain whether Sankavva was in fact a prostitute, or using a fierce metaphor for the conflict she felt between social propriety and ecstatic love. To assume her a prostitute based on a single lyric seems to miss the imagination so many bhakti poets have shown, and the assumption reduces her poem to a constrained literalism.

In my harlot's trade
having taken one man's money
I dare not accept a second man's, sir.
   And if I do,
   they'll strip me naked and
      kill me.

And if I lie down
   with someone polluted,
They'll sever my hands
   ears and nose with a
   red-hot knife, sir.

Ah, no,
knowing your reputation I will not.
This is my word,
   O god without shame.

*—Revised from the translation by Susan Daniels\**

* Tharu, Susie and K. Lalitas (eds) 1993. *Women Writing in India, Volume I: 600 BC to the Early Twentieth Century.* New Delhi: Oxford University Press.

# Telugu Poets

## Annamacharya

Annamacharya, or Annamaya as he is often called, started the tradition of devotional songs in the Telugu language. He was born in 1408 at Tallapaka village, in the Cuddapah district of Andhra Pradesh, to a *smarta* brahmin family. As a child he sang to Venkatesvara—the form of Visnu as Lord of the Tirumalai Hills—and sang so one-pointedly that his parents were dismayed, fearing he would become a mendicant. When still a child he experienced a dream in which, 'I saw Lord Venkatesvara, father of the cosmos, gazing on me.' He adds, in one of his compositions to the god, 'you gave your command, honoring my tongue with the chance to sing songs of praise to you.'

The Tirumalai Hills consist of seven peaks, said to resemble a coiled serpent. Near Seshacalam or Serpent Peak, sits the Tirumala Temple, seat of Venkatesvara. At age sixteen Annamaya set out for the temple as a pilgrim. Climbing the serried ranks of hills, at one point he lay down, fatigued, on a stone ledge in a bamboo thicket. In his sleep the Goddess Alamelumangamma, the god's consort, told him to remove his sandals and he would not tire as he climbed. She fed him *prasad* (left-over devotional food) from the temple, promising that her Lord would bless him when he arrived. Annamaya composed on the spot a *satakam*, or a hundred verses, of praise to her. The following day, finding that business had closed the temple doors before his arrival, Annamaya sang a spontaneous satakam to Venkatesvara, and the doors blew open for him.

Eventually Annamaya was placed in charge of temple singing, and received the title Grandfather Poet of the Padas. He composed at least one song a day, generally as he bathed in a nearby pool or waterfall. His son claimed that over the course of his life he had composed 32,000 *padas*, which were inscribed on copper plates. A storehouse of these coppers at the temple came to light in the second decade of the twentieth century—a collection of 14,000 of the songs.

A pada is a brief musical composition, sung in light classical mode. In the case of devotional compositions, they are sung as kirtan in the temple. Often temple dancers, the *devadasis*, will choreograph steps to the songs. In south India, it was Annamaya who gave the pada form a standardized cast, with an opening line, the *pallavai*, which recurs as a refrain or burden, sometimes with a second line, the *anupallavai*. The songs belong to the devadasis and their temple musicians. As with the Virasaiva poets of the Kannada tradition, the particular name of the god acts as a *mudra*, or identifying signature—contrasting with the northern tradition in which the poet's name identifies the composer.

Annamaya's genius led him to songs that are uttered in the voice of a courtesan, mistress, or wife of the god, while the deity is addressed as a wayward lover. The devotional song is cast as erotic, and with Annamaya and some of his successors, the line between prayer and love-song seems very thin indeed. This was a tradition in which the men composed songs, which were then performed—sung and danced—by women; the songs became part of the female repertoire. Annamaya's songs use the mudra Venkatesvara, while his successors have their own name for their god.

'Suvvi suvvi suvvi …'
    singing like this (at the temple festival)
      pearly-teeth girls with lovely smiles pound,
        (to mash rice in the mortar stone)

Like this the women become centred in their minds
repeating 'Ola! ola!' with joy, immersed in their love
The girls pound out the sound, again and again

using the glances of their eyes as pestles: 'Ola!'
    Suvvi suvvi suvvi …

The golden lacy borders of their silk saris sway when
they pound the rice this way saying 'Suvvi!'
the dangling silk rhythmically sways as they have fun
pounding together as a group in joyous unison 'Ola!'
    Suvvi suvvi suvvi …

Their loose long hair is swaying, and dangling garlands
swing from their abundant bouncing breasts
and the pretty women like half-blossomed flowers
are overflowing with beauty and they are pounding 'Ola!'
    Suvvi suvvi suvvi …

The tinkling of their bangles makes a *ghalghal* sound
the women with hands as soft as new leaves say 'Ola!'
their midriffs are pretty and their hips rock back and forth
the women pounding use their glances as pestles, 'Ola!'
    Suvvi suvvi suvvi …

The girls have an aura of the fragrance of camphor
and sweet flowers decorate this festival place
they sing praise of the Lord of the temple pool,
in love with him, full of desire for his love-play 'Ola!'
    Suvvi suvvi suvvi …
       singing like this (at the temple festival)
          pearly-teeth girls with lovely smiles
             pound, using their glances as pestles
                smashing rice in the mortar stone


What are these jasmine flowers for?
Tell him to wear them himself
For what am I but a tribal girl (*chenchu*)
my hairstyle has fragrance naturally

What would I do with this silk sari
Shiny green leaves are good enough for me

Give it back; tell him that he can wind it
as a sash around his waist—I'm tribal

What do I want with a bed with a canopy
Tell him to keep it and sleep on it
What am I but a chenchu girl who'd really
Rather roll around on the earth beneath a tree

*—Translated by William J. Jackson**

Don't you know my house,
the palace of the love god,
flooded with the sweet smell of flowers?

Don't you know the house
in the shade of the tamarind grove,
that narrow space between golden hills?

That's where you lose your senses,
where the love god hunts without fear.

  *Don't you know my house?*

Don't you know the house,
the love god's marketplace,
where the dark clears and yet does not clear?

Don't you know the house
where you live in your own heart?
That's where feelings hold court.

  *Don't you know my house?*

Don't you know the house
in the crazy garden?
You should know. You're the god on the hill.

* Jackson, William J. 1998. *Songs of Three Great South Indian Saints*. Delhi: Oxford University Press.

It's gates are sealed by the love god.
That's where you heap
all your wealth.

*Don't you know my house?*

—*Translated by V. Narayana Rao and David Shulman**

These marks of black musk
on her lips, red as buds,
what are they but letters of love
sent by our friend to her lover?

Her eyes the eyes of a *cakora* bird,
why are they red in the corners?

Think it over, my friends:
what is it but the blood
still staining the long glances
that pierced her beloved
after she drew them from his body
back to her eyes?

*What are they but letters of love?*

How is it that this woman's breasts
show so bright through her sari?

Can't you guess, my friends?
It's the rays from the crescents
left by the nails of her lover,
rays luminous as moonlight on a summer night?

*What are they but letters of love?*

---

* Ramanujan, A.K., Velchuru Narayana Rao, and David Shulman. 1994. *When God is a Customer: Telugu Courtesan Songs by Ksetrayya and Others.* Berkeley: University of California Press.

What are these graces,
these pearls,
raining down her cheeks?

Can't you imagine, friends?
What could they be but beads of sweat
left on her gentle face
by the god on the hill
when he pressed hard,
frantic from love?

*What are they but letters of love?*

—*Translated by Velcheru Narayana Rao and David Shulman**

# Dhurjati

Sometime in the middle of the sixteenth century the poet Dhurjati
arrived at the temple of Kalahasti in Andhra Pradesh. The grounds of the
temple lie on a bank of the river today called the Mogileru but known to
tradition by a Sanskrit name, Suvarnamukhari, River of Golden Sound.
The temple is dedicated to a local form of Siva, Srikalahastisvara, Lord
Kalahasti, whose name is comprised of words for spider, snake, and
elephant.

Of Dhurjati's life and teachings, little is known but the poetry.
He composed a long, ornate poem in Telugu—in the Sanskrit *kavya*
style—celebrating the Kalahasti Temple, recounting in detail the
legends connected with it. Tales of a spider, a snake, and an elephant
who showed their devotions to Siva, figure prominently. The poem's
colophon assigns the poem to Dhurjati, and the poem's elegant finish,

* Narayana Rao, Velcheru and David Shulman. 2005. *God on the Hill: Temple Poems from Tirupati*. New Delhi: Oxford University Press.

full of Sanskrit style compound-words, displays Dhurjati's training as a court poet. Tradition also assigns to him another collection, the *Kalahastisvara Satakamu*, or Hundred Poems to Lord Kalahasti, in which his disdain for the pride and pettiness of rulers is so pronounced it seems to confirm direct experience.

A satakam, a collection of a hundred poems, is a common form throughout India. Dozens if not hundreds occur in Sanskrit, Tamil, and many of the literary vernaculars. The number 100 is more symbolic than specific (the number 108, auspicious and emanating mystical powers, being a common number). Dhurjati's may hold 116 poems, though no modern scholar has produced a critical edition. Its poems continue to be chanted by Telugu speakers, who articulate its rhythms in a manner distinct to Telugu poetics. Tradition credits the poems to Dhurjati; though no old manuscript carries his name there's no reason to doubt he wrote it. His name, Dhurjati, Twisted Locks (or wearer of twisted hair), places him with the Saivites. Siva and the sadhus dedicated to him still wear dreadlocks, twisted into ropes, matted with cow dung or ash.

In the colophon to his long ornate poem Dhurjati calls himself *bhaviparanmukha*, 'opposed to those who get reborn', meaning the deluded who don't worship Siva. His translators take the 116 poems to Lord Kalahasti as an emotional autobiography. He can be angry, obstinate, bitter, disdainful, terrified, or occasionally ecstatic, though rapture is not a common mood. 'Many of the poems … show the deep imprint of personal experience in the quality of their imagery and the intensity of their feeling,' the translators write. The poems 'have long been used in the Telugu country, among those who know them by heart, as means of focusing on their own emotions, in time of confusion, trouble, or joy'. The arrogance of political rulers, the futility of prestige or wealth, the constraint of family, the baffling unfairness of life—potent realism and a deeper fatalism twist through Dhurjati's lyrics. He is also explicit about poetry as his spiritual calling, and about the indifference of materialistic people.

> I have labeled myself your poet,
> and tying a string around my wrist
> I keep it there as a sign,
> but this vow has no worth
> that the world values.

## From the Kalahastisvara Satakamu

My chest has been worn away
by the breasts of women rubbing against it.
My skin has been roughened
with love scars from their nails.
Lost in the straining of passion, youth
has gone.
My hair has started falling out,
I'm sick of it all.
I can't go on in this circling world,
God of Kalahasti, make me
                              desireless.                              (1)

So long as I am serving you,
let catastrophes come to me
or endless festivals,
let people call me
just an ordinary man or let them
praise me as a great saint,
let me be deluded by the pleasures of the world
or let Knowledge become mine,
let the movements of the planets
pull me down
or let sweet things happen!
Could any of it mark me,
O God of Kalahasti?                                                  (3)

Those kings drunk with power,
serving them is like being in hell.
The things they give you—women with eyes
like lotuses, palanquins, horses, jewels—
all breed pain.
I've had enough of wanting them.
O God of Kalahasti, through your grace
change me so that I awaken
to the wealth that is Illumination.                                  (6)

Waves, trembling leaves,
glittering mirrors, lamps
in a wind, the flickering
ears of an elephant, vision after vision
of imaginary water, firefly light,
letters written on air, a single breath,
rice balls made of the milk of moonlight—
such is wealth.
Then why do men go blind with pride
about it,
O God of Kalahasti? (8)

Is that cave of pleasure filled with dirt
the doorway to *the susumna*?
And the hair around it, is that *kundalini*?
Are feet, hands, and eyes *the six cakras*?
Is the face *the supreme cakra*
or the forehead *the crescent of the moon*?
Is making love *yoga*?
O God of Kalahasti,
why do men wear themselves out after women? (14)

Saying this is your wife, they bring a woman
and the knots are tied at the neck.
Then children come one after another
and the boys take their brides
and the girls are given in marriage.
O God of Kalahasti,
how did you fashion this worthless wheel
of family love that turns us,
cog meshing smoothly with cog around
and around? (23)

Even if I were to sleep
with the women of heaven,
desire would not weaken
in the slightest.
Even if I were to gain

the power of the Creator,
I could not satisfy
my greed.
Even if I were to swallow every one of the worlds,
my wild, deep-seated rage
would not cease.
In these, there are no pleasures
that I desire.
O God of Kalahasti,
through service to you I will cross over
the great ocean of my faults. (40)

When mourners cry over the dead
burning on the river banks, they will say,
'O God of Death! We are coming,
we as well, you can be sure of us,
we know it!' Then they take the cleansing bath
and the fools move on and they forget
the real weight of what they have said,
O God of Kalahasti. (42)

If I should pray to those worms who are kings,
would the suffering of the living
go away as it only can
through worshipping your feet?
Can the pain of a child's hunger be soothed
by sucking the dewlap of a goat,
O God of Kalahasti, instead of the breast
of the mother who gives him her milk
with love in her eyes? (43)

How can you be praised in elaborate language,
similes, conceits, overtones, secondary meanings,
or textures of sound? They cannot contain
your form. Enough of them!
More than enough. Can poetry hold out
before the face of truth?
Ah, but we poets,

O God of Kalahasti,
why don't we feel any shame?                                    (49)

What they call bad dreams,
omens, conjunctions of planets,
readings of palms, what they call
diseases caused by magic
or the evil eye, malevolent spirits,
all the varieties of poison,
how many traps
have you made for living beings
and still given them love
for their lives which cannot last longer
than the blink of an eye,
O God of Kalahasti?                                            (52)

Why is it some people think of killing other
people and taking over their thrones?
Won't they die themselves, won't their wealth
leave them? Will they live eternally
with their wives and their friends and their sons?
Isn't death, O God of Kalahasti,
O isn't it coming
some day?                                                      (61)

It's a simple thing to be a guru
and graciously say to your disciples, 'Here, take
this water I have used to bathe
my lotus-like feet. Your money,
your body, your life all
belong to me, your guru,'
but to be contemptuous of wealth
and through the way of non-action,
O God of Kalahasti,
to make you
      rise up in the mind,
that is a difficult thing even
for a learned man.                                             (71)

I have attended to spells
and magic rituals,
I have been instructed
in the secrets of Sankhya and Yoga.
I have recited the Vedas and the shastras.
But my doubts have not been answered
even as much as a mustard seed
set down next to a pumpkin.
Give me faith,
O God of Kalahasti,
show me the way
to firm, stable knowledge.                                    (77)

No more than a handful of water
or a single flower
for your hair,
offered with stable devotion
on this earth by a human being
can in the end bring him
the holy Ganges, the crescent moon
and you.
O God of Kalahasti,
for isn't your glory
all this vast world?                                          (95)

In town after town,
men who sing ordinary songs
now call themselves poets.
They go into places and explain their
        songs to somebody
they happen to find
and they say to them,
'You are aesthetes! You know poetry!'
O God of Kalahasti,
substance and emptiness are not distinguished.
Poetry has been cheapened.
Where is it
good poets can go?                                            (105)

I have had my satisfaction
with pleasures at the doorway of the King of Love
and those who have come to me through entering
the palace gates of many kings.
Now I want quiet. Show me
the doorway to the highest truth
where, through your kindness,
O God of Kalahasti,
I can be at ease and rest.                                          (108)

*—Translated by Hank Heifetz and V. Narayana Rao**

# Ksetrayya

The translators of Ksetrayya regard him as 'the most versatile and central
of the Telugu *padam* poets', but add that virtually no biographical
details are known. From his songs, which name several rulers—no doubt
patrons for whom he composed—he clearly lived in the mid-seventeenth
century. His mudra, or signature, is Muvva Gopala—Cowherd of
Muvva village, near Kuchipudi, where the Kuchipudi dance tradition is
centred. One of his padams claims he sang thousands of poems for each
of several patrons, but only about four hundred come down to us.

Ksetrayya sang to many gods besides Muvva Gopala, and the range
of deities has prompted some to interpret his name (Sanskrit *Ksetra-jña*)
as 'knower of sacred places'. Based on an oral tradition, a number of
stories portray a wandering bhakti poet, moving from temple to temple
for the purpose of honouring the gods with song. His translators believe
he was more likely a poet of the courts and royal towns of the Nayaka
rulers. 'We see him,' they write, 'as a poet composing for, and with
the assumed persona of, the sophisticated and cultured courtesans who
performed before gods and kings.' It is clear in Ksetrayya's more explicit

* Heifetz, Hank and Velcheru Narayana Rao. 1987. *For the Lord of the Animals:
Poems from the Telugu.* Berkeley: University of California Press.

lyrics that the singer's persona is a courtesan or even a more common prostitute, who speaks to the god as though he were a patron. Based on these lyrics, the translators titled their book of Telugu poetry *When God is a Customer.*

With Ksetrayya the bhakti tradition merges so seamlessly into explicit sexual description that the question has to come up: are these devotional songs in the guise of erotic folk poetry, or love songs lightly masked as devotional?

## A Young Woman to a Friend

Those women, they deceived me.
They told me he was a woman,
and now my heart is troubled
by what he did.

First I thought
she was my aunt and uncle's daughter,
so I bow to her, and she blesses me:
'You'll get married soon,
don't be bashful. *I* will bring you
the man of your heart.'

'Those firm little breasts of yours
will soon
grow round and full,' she says.

And she fondles them
and scratches them
with the edge of her nail.

'Come eat with me,' she says,
as she holds me close
and feeds me as at a wedding.

*Those women, they told me he was a woman!*

Then she announces:
'My husband is not in town.

Come home with me.'
So I go and sleep in her bed.

After a while she says,
'I'm bored. Let's play
a kissing game, shall we?
Too bad we're both women.'

Then, as she sees me fall asleep,
off my guard,
she tries some
strange things on me.

*Those women, they told me she was a woman!*

She says, 'I can't sleep.
Let's do what men do.'
Thinking 'she' was a woman,
I get on top of him.

Then he doesn't let go:
he holds me so tight
he loses himself in me.
Wicked as ever he declares:

'I am your Muvva Gopala!'
And he touches me expertly
and makes love to me.

*Those women, they told me he was a woman!*


## The Courtesan Speaks to Her Lover

I'm seeing you at last.
It's been four or five months,
Muvva Gopala!

Last night in my dream
you took shape before my eyes.
I got up with a start,

looked for you,
didn't find you.
The top of my sari
was soaked with tears.
I turned to water,
gave in to sorrow.
I asked myself
if you might not
be thinking of me, too.

*I'm seeing you at last,*
       *the answer to my prayers*

Ever since we parted,
there's been no betel for me,
no food,
no fun,
no sleep.
I'm like a lone woman
in a forest
after sunset,
soaked through by the rain
in the heavy dark,
unable to find a way.

*I'm seeing you at last,*
       *the answer to my prayers*

My parents blame me,
my girlfriends mock.
This may sound strange,
but I can tell you:
ever since we first made love,
my world
has become you.
I have no mind
other than yours.

*I'm seeing you at last,*
       *the answer to my prayers*

# A Married Woman to Her Lover

Go find a root or something.
I have no girlfriends here I can trust.

When I swore at you, you didn't listen.
You said all my curses were blessings.
You grabbed me, you bastard,
and had me by force.
I've now missed my period,
and my husband is not in town.

*Go find a root or something*

I have set myself up for blame.
What's the use of blaming you?
I've even lost my taste for food.
What can I do now?
Go to the midwives and get me a drug
before the women begin to talk.

*Go find a root or something*

As if he fell from the ceiling,
my husband is suddenly home.
He made love to me last night.
Now I fear no scandal.
All my wishes, Muvva Gopala,
have reached their end,
so, in your image,
I'll bear you a son.

*Go find a root or something*

# A Woman to Her Lover

How soon it's morning already!
There's something new in my heart,
Muvva Gopala.

Have we talked even a little while
to undo the pain of our separation till now?
You call me in your passion, 'Woman, come to me,'
and while your mouth is still on mine,

> *it's morning already!*

Caught in the grip of the Love God,
angry with him, we find release drinking
at each other's lips.

You say, 'My girl, your body is tender as a leaf,'
and before you can loosen your tight embrace,

> *it's morning already!*

Listening to my moans as you touch certain spots,
the pet parrot mimics me, and O how we laugh in bed!

You say, 'Come close, my girl,'
and make love to me like a wild man, Muvva Gopala,
and as I get ready to move on top,

> *it's morning already!*

> *—Translated by A.K. Ramanujan, V. Narayana Rao,*
> *and David Shulman\**

# Sarangapani

Only two hundred padams by this poet survive. His translators write:
'He is linked with the little kingdom of Karvetinagaram in the Chittoor
district of southern Andhra and with the minor ruler Makaraju Venkata
Perumal Raju (d. 1732).'

* Ramanujan, A.K., Velchuru Narayana Rao, and David Shulman. 1994.
*When God is a Customer: Telugu Courtesan Songs by Ksetrayya and Others.* Berkeley:
University of California Press.

# To an Older Woman

All those days he called you,
you were too proud.
Now you're circling
his house.

Are you in love,
after you're past
the age for men?
Don't be coquettish now.
All those days Venugopala called you,
you were too proud.

*Now you're circling his house*

Hasn't your face
hardened with age?
Pale lips,
wobbling rows of teeth,
body lusterless,
beauty dulled.
But all those days that kind man
fell at your feet and begged,
you were too proud.

*Now you're circling his house*

Look at you:
half your hair is gray.
You barely look like a woman.
Forty, and nearsighted,
you don't have breath enough to sing.
All those days that handsome man
begged you not to be cross,
you were too proud.

*Now you're circling his house*

You've cleaned up
your place of love
and made it look new.
You've come alone
at this time of night
on this lonely path.
If Venugopala does you the favor
of sleeping with you,
won't people laugh?

*Now you're circling his house*

—*Translated by A.K. Ramanujan, V. Narayana Rao,*
*and David Shulman**

* Ramanujan, A.K., Velchuru Narayana Rao, and David Shulman. 1994. *When God is a Customer: Telugu Courtesan Songs by Ksetrayya and Others*. Berkeley: University of California Press.

# WEST

# Varkaris

## Jnandev

Born in 1275 in Maharashtra, Jnandev is best known for his *Jnaneshvari*, a poetic commentary on the Bhagavadgita. He is considered the first of the Varkari poets, their 'arch-mentor and preceptor' in the words of translator Dilip Chitre. Deliberately breaking with the Sanskrit literary tradition of the day (in which he had composed his earlier commentaries), and rejecting the dictates of his own brahminic upbringing, Jnandev composed songs in the folk metres of the illiterate local people.

Jnandev's father had been a disciple of Ramanand, but married and became a householder. Ostracized by the brahmin authorities, he and his wife were pressured into suicide as penance. The couple's four children—Nivritti, Jnandev, Sopan, and their younger sister Muktabai—continued to be treated as pariahs until they had proved their spiritual accomplishment. This they did through debate with the brahmins, and through a series of brilliant compositions, including the *Jnaneshvari*. Jnandev refuted the superiority of the brahmins, largely through what became the central belief of the Varkaris: god is not separate from the world, in all its manifestations.

For his vernacular songs Jnandev drew on two folk traditions. The first is the *ovi*, a song used by women when working with mortar and pestle, or at the *rahat*, a Persian-style water wheel. Most ovi lyrics are more protest song than work song—complaints about hard work, complaints about marriage, and the patriarchal structure of the family, and they often call upon a deity who might deliver them from servility.

The other song pattern Jnandev used is the *abhang*, a style of call-and-response used for spiritual occasions, epic stories, and the sort. The abhang is generally sung as a solo performance, with an audience joining the singer in the refrain or burden. Both ovi and abhang were used in religious kirtan, which Chitre describes as 'a several-hours-long live folk theatre presentation'. Jnandev drew on the stories of Krishna for his songs. Besides the affectionate term Vitthal, he used the names Hari and Govinda, as well as depicting his deity as a 'blue cowherd'.

Jnandev completed his life on earth at age twenty-two. He descended into an underground vault in the Vithoba temple at Alandi near the modern city of Pune, and entered a particular trance, the *sanjeevan samadhi*. Most likely he learnt the technique from Nath yogins. The town of Alandi has since become one of the three major pilgrimage destinations for the Maharashtrian devotees of Vithoba, along with Pandharpur, where Vithoba's principal temple sits, and Dehu, birthplace of Tukaram.

Blue is this sky, a blue filled with love,
Blue is this entire symmetry.

A blue being-in-itself, the blue of all *karma*,
I see a blue *Guru* in his blue resort.

Bluely I behave, I eat blue,
I see blueness in a blue sort of way.

Jnandev has entered the loving embrace
Of the blue cowherd in the school of blue.


The quintessence of awareness,
The knowledge of infinity,
The one whom the sky clothes,
Who has no form, no colour, nor property:

That graceful One, Hari, the reliever:
I've seen Him filling my eyes!
Seeing Him, I've set aside
Even the act of seeing!

Says Jnandev, inside any flame is
The Self's very own flame:
And that flame is imaged here
Standing on The Brick!


Shall I call you the formed One?
Shall I call you the formless?
The formed and the unformed is
Only the one Govind!

He cannot be deduced
He cannot be conceived
*The Shrutis* say,
*'He's not such; nor even such.'*

Shall I call You the vastest One?
Shall I call you the minutest One?
The vast and the minute
Are only One Govind.

Shall I call You the visible One?
Shall I call You the invisible One?
Both the visible and the invisible
Are the only One Govind.

By the blessing of Nivrutti,
Jnanadev speaks,
'Our great parent, husband of the Goddess Rakhuma, is
Vitthal.'

*—Translated by Dilip Chitre**


* Chitre, Dilip. 2008b. *Poets of Vithoba: Anthology of Marathi Bhakti Poetry.* Unpublished manuscript.

# Namdev

Born to a tailor and his wife in the village of Narasvami, Maharashtra, Namdev moved to Pandharpur shortly after, as his parents were devotees of Vithoba. At the age of two, Namdev uttered his first word, 'Vitthal', and as he grew up, could think only of the deity. This account conflicts with another that claims he joined a gang as a youth. In this latter tale, he killed a man in a brawl, then became steeped in remorse hearing the laments of the man's wife. Shortly after, he saw a vision of Vithoba, and became the foremost member of the Varkari Panth, or 'path of the Varkaris'. He never took particularly to tailoring, and showed no aptitude or interest in either work or money. He married—unhappily it seems, as his wife had a worldly cast of mind—and fathered four children. After his vision of Vithoba, the second great event of his life was when he met Jnandev, a few years his junior, and the two set off on lengthy pilgrimages, entering Rajasthan, with tales of miracles attending them.

Along with Jnandev, Eknath, and Tukaram, Namdev is regarded as one of the four great poets of Vithoba. Once, in an abhang, he made an impulsive pledge to compose a billion poems for Vitthal, just as Valmiki had composed a monumental work of 'a billion' verses to Rama. Vithoba tried to intercede. The vow is impossible to fulfil, claimed Vithoba, noting that in the degenerate present age human life is far too brief to compose so many poems. Three hundred years later, at the outset of his own life in bhakti, Tukaram dreamt that Namdev appeared, asking that he 'write those from the billion I haven't completed'. The comical nature of this request shouldn't obscure the fact of spiritual companionship, between two poets separated by three centuries.

The other Marathi poet he influenced was Janabai, who by the testimony of her own abhangs lived in Namdev's house, as a maid or nursemaid to the family.

Namdev's poems often erode the distinction between creeds. Some have found a place amid the Sikh sacred books, and Namdev's visions of Vithoba also merge with Siva, or with Krishna as the pastoralist figure Gopal.

I was born in a family of tailors
But my motive was threaded
Into *Sadashiva*
The ever pure spirit of the universe!

*Shiva* at night, *Shiva* at day, I sewed on,
My heart beat for *Shiva*
But found
No rest.

*Sadashiva*, my ever-sewing needle,
*Sadashiva*, my endless thread;
*Sadashiva* my cloth, my hectic pair of scissors, my given measure—
My entire work of tailoring was *Sadashiva*.

Says Nama,
I found
The ever-pure *Shiva* to my heart's content
Embodied in *Vithoba*.


The dark rain-cloud fills the sky.
Oh my mother!
He is encircled
By lightning and thunder!

I can't wait to see
Govind, my cowherd!
How sweet is this
Rain!

The peacocks dance
In spontaneous joy.
Their throats turn blue
With love.

Nama sees his Lord
With such pure vision!
Oh my mother!
My soul belongs to Gopal!

The night is black. The water pot is black.
Oh my mother!
The waters of the Yamuna
Are black, too.

The veil is black. The jewel is black.
Oh my mother!
The pearls I wear around my neck
Are also black.

I am black. My breasts are clothed in black.
Oh my mother!
The waist-knot of my sari is
Also black.

The maiden lover
Goes alone to the river.
O my mother! Send her the black image of her lover
As company!

Nama, the servant of *Vishnu,*
Has a black mistress. Oh my mother!
How black can the image of Krishna
Be?

*—Translated by Dilip Chitre**

* Chitre, Dilip. 2008b. *Poets of Vithoba: Anthology of Marathi Bhakti Poetry.*
Unpublished manuscript.

# Muktabai

Muktabai, reputed to be beautiful and profoundly accomplished as a yogini, was Jnandev's younger sister. With her three brothers, Nivritti, Jnandev, and Sopan, she founded the Varkari tradition. After their parents' death, Nivritti, the eldest, became guru to the other three. He had been initiated into Nath yoga practices, and Mukta learnt from his instruction both the mystic practices and that riddle-like language the Nath tradition uses to conceal its teachings from non-initiates. It is this terminology that makes Mukta's abhangs particularly hard to unravel, and some get referred to as riddles.

Once when her brother, Jnandev, had been abused by a brahmin, he locked himself into a room. Mukta in a series of verses urges him to come out. She tells him first that god's spirit is everywhere, even in unpleasant people, and second, that Varkaris do not hide from life. Nowhere does she sing about hardship in her birth as a woman, though like her brothers she spurns orthodoxy and caste. Evidently she never married but lived with her brothers.

Mukta became the guru of Changdev, a highly accomplished Tantric yogin, far older than her. In one of her strangest songs she takes the role of a mother, addressing the elderly Changdev as an infant. He in turn refers to her as guru, and in one verse describes her 'eating cooked diamonds'—a reference to her yogic powers. At the age of eighteen she took *samadhi*, vanishing in a flash of lightning. This of course may refer to her mystical powers; a song of Jnandev's describes her encounter with Goroba, another yogin of the period.

*The powder of pearls was thrown in the skies. There was a brilliant flash of lightning. The sky was clothed in beautiful purple. The brilliant blue point began to dance. In a dazzling thunder, the lightning disappeared in itself. Muktai met Goroba. In that meeting, says Jnandev, Self-knowledge came to be known.*

(translation by Ruth Vanita)

When one looks beyond the void,
There is not even a void left.

The one who sees keeps what's seen
In one's own place.

O mother mine! What a great saviour this!
The One who illuminates All!
He appeared in Pandharpur
Bringing *Vaikunth* down with Himself!

One does not know where He will go—
Being, becoming, and vanishing at will!
The resonance of *The Shrutis* is thus realized:
'*Not such is the One; nor such is the One.*'

Muktai is filled with love.
Vitthal amazes her.
The mattress is emptiness.
Lie down upon emptiness.


'Where the origin of resonance merges with the nucleus of light,
The speech of the living expresses the One Lord of Being.

Needless temptations pave all the ways of the world
And that's the realm of death and veritable hell.'

His words are addressed to those
Who are mere creatures the Lord created.

Nivrutti's advice to Muktai is simple:
From here on, we have no world to chase.

*—Translated by Dilip Chitre**

* Chitre, Dilip. 2008b. *Poets of Vithoba: Anthology of Marathi Bhakti Poetry*. Unpublished manuscript.

# Janabai

The daughter of shudra parents, Janabai seems to have lost her own family early. She entered the household of Namdev's father, Damsheti, when young, and grew up there as a servant. Often ambiguously signing her verses *Namyachi Jani* (Jani of Namdev), it is hard to tell whether she regards the older Varkari as her beloved teacher or her employer. Namdev, renowned for his ambitious vow to compose a billion verses to Vithoba, divided the work among his household. Even Janabai received an allotment. She, of course, 'falls in the category of those *sants* whose low social status distanced them from the religious establishment,' writes Ruth Vanita, 'but whom god is believed to have favoured more highly than the rich and powerful.' In her verses Vithoba helps her with backbreaking chores; he 'has gathered cow-dung with Janabai', wrote Tukaram 300 years later.

Janabai's excruciating awareness of being a shudra, an orphan, a woman, and a servant, come out in her songs. At times she appears pleased to have at least entered service with a family of bhaktas: 'being the servant of Namdev who is immersed in love for Vithoba, Jani shares in the joy.' Mostly her verses reveal hard, thankless work though, and there are tales of mistreatment by Namdev's mother, the matron of the house. The distinctiveness of Janabai's vision is that she often pictures Vithoba leaving his temple and coming to protect her from abuse, or to assist her in her labours. Pounding and grinding grain, washing clothes, gathering fuel, making cow-dung cakes—'Jani says, my Vithalabai does such low work for my sake!'

That name *Vithalabai*—coined by Jana—attaches the feminine suffix —*bai* or 'sister' to Vithal's name. The god comes, sometimes as a male, sometimes a female, and removes lice from Jana's scalp, or washes and oils her hair, as a female companion or a boyfriend might. With this special relationship to her god, Janabai can sing of abandoning shame along with social convention, and in one of her best known abhangs says, 'I've become a slut for you, Keshav.' In another memorable lyric, she asks the celebrated Varkari poet Jnandev to enter her womb: 'Stay with Dasi (servant) Jani, birth after birth.'

Jani sweeps with a broom
The Lord loads up the garbage

He carries it in a basket on His head
Throws it away in a distant dump

So much under the spell of *Bhakti* is He
He now performs the lowliest tasks

Says Jani to Vithoba
How shall I return Your favours?

*—Translated by Dilip Chitre\**

Cast off all shame,
and sell yourself
in the marketplace;
then alone
can you hope
to reach the Lord.

Cymbals in hand,
a *veena* upon my shoulder,
I go about;
who dares to stop me?

The pallav of my sari
falls away (A scandal!);
yet will I enter
the crowded marketplace
without a thought.

Jani says, My Lord
I have become a slut
to reach Your home.

*—Translated by Vilas Sarang†*

* Chitre, Dilip. 2008b. *Poets of Vithoba: Anthology of Marathi Bhakti Poetry.* Unpublished manuscript.
† My paraphrases from poems translated by Vilas Sarang in Anne Feldhaus, *Images of Women in Maharashtrion Literature and Religion.* Ithaca, New York: state University of New York Press, 1996.

Jani has had enough of samsara,
but how will I repay my debt?

You leave your greatness behind you
to grind and pound with me.

O Lord you become a woman
washing me and my soiled clothes,

proudly you carry the water
and gather dung with your own two hands.

O Lord, I want
a place at your feet,
says Jani, Namdev's dasi.


If the Ganga flows to the ocean
and the ocean turns her away,
tell me, O Vitthal,
who would hear her complaint?

Can the river reject its fish?
Can the mother spurn her child?

Jani says,
Lord,
you must accept those
who surrender to you.

*—Translated by Sarah Sellergren*[*]


Jani loosens her hair
Among basil plants growing wild

The Lord with butter in the palm of His hand
Gently massages her head

* Feldhaus, Anne (ed.) 1996. *Images of Woman in Maharashtrian Literature and Religion*. Ithaca, New York: State University of New York Press.

My poor little Jani has no one but me
He thinks as he pours water on her head

Jani tells all the folks
My boy-friend gives me a shower

*—Translated by Dilip Chitre\**

# Chokhamela

Chokhamela was by birth a *mahar*, a remover of dead animals from
the towns. Though he is said to be from Mangalvedha, his polluted
status required him to live outside the precincts of the town, being an
outcaste and considered by caste Hindus a defilement. An outcaste
has no place in the Hindu social fabric, and Chokha would have been
denied schooling, access to literature or scripture, use of the village well
or fields, and entry to the temple.

Legend tells that Chokhamela made the traditional religious journey
to Pandharpur, where he heard Namdev singing abhangs in a kirtan
celebration. Overcome with love for Vithoba he pledged himself as one
of Namdev's students. Through Namdev's intercession Chokha got
access to the outer grounds of Vithoba's temple, but brahmin priests
refused to allow him inside the gates. 'Chokha's habitual place seems
to have been at the outer doors of the temple,' writes his translator,
Rohini Mokashi-Punekar. 'His poems quite simply and humbly refer
to his standing there,' she adds, 'quite without self-pity and certainly
without rancour.'

There exist no historical records regarding Chokhamela. But his
lowly social stature and exclusion from even basic rights gave rise to
stories of a sort of anti-hero bhakti poet. In some tales Vithoba even

* Chitre, Dilip. 2008b. *Poets of Vithoba: Anthology of Marathi Bhakti Poetry.*
Unpublished manuscript.

leaves his own temple to fetch Chokha, carry him inside, embrace and caress him, and in a casteless utopian gesture, even eats with him.

Chokha died, the tales say, when a section of a fort wall he was building in his home town with other mahar labourers collapsed, burying a group of workers. Namdev, hearing of his student's death, went in search of the remains. Despite the many mutilated bodies, crushed under the wall's rubble, he was able to locate Chokhamela's bones: he heard them whispering, 'Vitthal, Vitthal'. Namdev transported the bones to Pandharpur and buried them outside the main temple gates—at the exact spot Chokhamela had stood day after day in worship. Today a shrine marks his burial.

Chokhamela's abhangs include references to other Varkaris: Jnanesvar the rebellious brahmin, Namdev the tailor, Gora the potter, Savata the gardener, Janabai the nursemaid, Joga the oil presser, Sena the barber. 'Abhangs,' writes Mokashi-Punekar, 'are oral literature and as such there exists no final and completely authoritative edition of Chokhamela's poetry.' She observes that the impulse of the songs is spiritual, not literary. They belong to a community of bhaktas, the singing Varkaris, all of whom took personally the exclusion of any member of their spiritual family.

Why have you thrown
this challenge god?
Solve this riddle of mine;
enter my shoes, know
in your own self:
an outcaste,
what rights do I enjoy?
Says Chokha,
this low born
human body every
one drives away.
Doubts prey
on my mind,
what
can I do?

You know, Keshiraj, on the other hand,
I am filled with surprise.
A throne for one,
a hovel for another,
yet one other wanders bare.
One half-fed, another feasting,
for some not a scrap for the asking;
high glory for one,
good posts for a few,
others beg from village to village.
Such, it seems,
is the law of your world.
Says Chokha,
Hari, my fate lies in this.

A Vaishnav's house
feeds a dog, a pig
or a cat. My
heart is content:
won't beg
for any more pity. I
will gulp the leavings
on the slab of stone
outside
the house and lie
satisfied.
Says Chokha
I prostrate myself
to any
one going to
Pandhari.

At my wits end
now that the end
is here;
my life was spent in paying for

the past.
Where is the strength now
to attend others,
or to know
the empty snarls of desire. No
point in raising a cry:
all that I ever did
is only chaff.
Entangled in this mirage, what
a waste this mess of yours and mine.
Says Chokha
there is no way out:
there's nothing I understand.

The sugarcane is crooked,
but not its juice.
The bow is curved,
not the arrow.
The river is bent,
but not its water.
Chokha is twisted,
not his faith.
Why are you drawn
to the shape of a thing.

What drought has brought
this hungering that
you must for Jani
be at the pestle
grinding the grain.
Hungry you eat her dry
crumbs five or seven days
old. On that broken down cot, you make a dais
of her ragged quilt and there
you lie deep in sleep. He is
my lord, says Chokha,

early he wakes to bring
the cow dung in.

—*Translated by Rohini Mokashi-Punekar**

# Tukaram

Little undisputed factual material on Tukaram's life has come down
to the present. Because he was born a shudra, at the bottom of the
caste hierarchy, the lack of biographical material is unsurprising. That
Tukaram would write religious poems, and do so in Marathi, put him
at odds with the orthodox brahmins of his day, who considered it an
infraction simply for a shudra to voice any opinion on spiritual matters.
A vivid legend about Tuka gives a glimpse into religious tensions of
his day. Dilip Chitre writes: 'He was eventually forced to throw his
manuscripts into the local Indrayani river at Dehu, his native village, and
was presumably told by his mocking detractors that if indeed he were
a true devotee of God, then God would restore his sunken notebooks.'
Tukaram sat by the riverside, praying and fasting, and after thirteen days
his notebooks of poetry surfaced, undamaged by water.

The Vithoba temple at Dehu has on display a Tukaram manuscript
not only said to be written in his hand, but to be the one miraculously
restored from the waters. It contains 250 poems, though at the beginning
of the twentieth century it was recorded as holding around 700. No
scholar has compiled a full edition of the 8,000 poems in various ways
attributed to Tukaram, and the one official edition produced in 1873
under auspices of the Bombay Government bears 4,607 verses, in
numbered sequence.

Tukaram was born into a family of traders that owned a sizeable piece
of agricultural land on the bank of the Indrayani at Dehu. Coming from
a prosperous family of traders meant Tuka learnt to read and write, well

* Mokashi-Punekar, Rohini. 2002. *On the Threshold: Songs of Chokhamela*. New
Delhi: The Book Review Literary Trust.

enough at least to continue the family business. However, by the time he was twenty-one years old he had witnessed the death of his parents, his older brother, his wife, and his children, his beloved first wife dying in the great famine of 1629. Though he remarried, he lost all interest in trading, farming, and family life. He fell into debt, and began to go into the surrounding wilderness alone for long periods of time. At some point he turned his troubled attention and affections to Vitthal—his family's hereditary deity—and when at home dedicated himself to restoring a neglected and dilapidated shrine on his family estate. He disregarded his wife's reasonable pleas to return to work and to support the family, and many thought he'd gone mad. This second wife appears in many poems as a chief antagonist.

During this period, Vitthal and the fourteenth-century Varkari poet Namdev approached Tuka in a dream, initiating him into the tradition of abhang composition. Namdev, who during his own life had made the vow to compose one billion abhangs, then distributed part of the duty to other Varkaris, asked Tukaram to complete the task. Rather than giving Tuka conviction and delight, though, the dream threw him into despair. He had no direct experience of God apart from the dream, and was too honest to simply sing praise songs. This is what makes Tuka's poems so existential and in the end so appealing. They feel like the singular quest of a rigorously honest man. Dilip Chitre asks, 'How was he going to praise something that he had not experienced himself? He had been an honest trader. He vouched for the quality of every item sold … To him all poetry was empirical and so was religion. Experience or "realization" was the crucial test.'

At about the age of thirty Tukaram dreamt that as he was walking down to the river a yogin confronted him, placed a hand on his head, and gave him the mantra, *Rama Krishna Hari*. This seems to have been his second initiation, and the one that gave him entry to the ecstasy of the mystics. Tuka felt himself come utterly alive under Babaji's hand. Was it an enlightenment experience? In a more sceptical telling, this legend seems an attempt to Sanskritize Tuka, providing him a proper Guru out of a more orthodox, brahmin tradition.

At the age of forty-one Tukaram vanished. Devotees believe he was absorbed into light while singing his poetry on the bank of a river. The more hard-headed speculate that his enemies could have murdered him. His last poems suggest that he might have simply taken farewell of his friends and fellow villagers, and for unknown reasons set out, destination unknown, with no plan to return. In the late poems he tells his friends that from this point on, only 'talk about Tuka' would remain among them.

> I was only dreaming
> Namdeo and Vitthal
> Stepped into my dream
>
> 'Your job is to make poems,'
> said Namdeo,
> 'Stop fooling around.'
>
> Vitthal gave me the measure
> And slapped me gently
> To arouse me
> From my dream
> Within a dream
>
> 'The grand total
> Of the poems Namdeo vowed to write
> Was one billion,'
> He said,
> 'All the unwritten ones, Tuka,
> Are your dues.'

> This is really extraordinary, O Hari,
> You are supposed to relieve misery;
> And here I am, your own devotee,
> Whose house is haunted by poetry.
>
> The more I excel in poems praising you,
> The more my work seems flawed:
> This is yet another amazing paradox.
> Watchfulness is rewarded with anxiety.
>
> Says Tuka, My Lord, it's just dawned on me:
> To serve you is the ultimate difficulty.

Some of you may say
I am the author
Of these poems.
But
Believe me
This voice
Is not my own.

I have no
Personal skill.
It is
The Cosmic One
Making me speak.

What does a poor fellow like me
Know of the subtleties of meaning?
I speak what Govind
Makes me say.

He has appointed me
To measure it out.
The authority rests
With the Master; Not me.

Says Tuka, I'm only the servant.
See?
All this bears
The seal of His Name.


Why should I set up this shop
And mind its business?
Why should I advertise it
Making such a high pitch?

What's one small soul to you
That you would run to my rescue?
Isn't it futile to hope
That mouthing mere words would reveal you?

A king may not grant land to the landless;
But wouldn't he at least ensure
That his subjects get a meal?
After all a king must protect
The myth of his benevolence.

Don't you see the point, O Lord?
If you refuse me, says Tuka,
I'd be forced to close down your shop.


Insects in a fig
Cannot imagine
Worlds other than the fig.

There are so many fig-trees
In these woods:
And so many more
Vast clusters of stars.

To each his own is
Brahman
—Absolute Being.

How many such astral eggs
Will there be?

The Vast One bristles
With hairs
Of infinity.

Then there's the Vast One who contains
Trillions of vast ones.

The same One is
Nanda's loved little son—
Krishna
—The Infant Bliss Infinite.

When Tuka experiences
That bliss,
God's poetry enters
His small head.

## Advice to an Angry Wife

'Now there's nothing left for you to eat.
Will you eat your own children?
My husband is God-crazy!

'See how he beats his own head?
See how he wears garlands!
He has stopped minding his shop.

'His own belly is full
While the rest of us must starve

'Look at him striking cymbals
And opening his grotesque mouth
To sing to his God in his shrine!'

Says Tuka, be patient, my woman!
This is only the beginning!

## Advice to an Angry Wife

'He can't stand the idea of work;
He is used to getting free meals.

'As soon as he wakes, he starts to sing.
All hell breaks loose after that.

'These fellows are the living dead.
They have no conscience to prick.

'They've turned a blind eye to their families.
They have deserted their homes.

'Their wives twist and turn for them
While they crush their lives with a stone.'

Says Tuka, that's a good one, my wife!
Here! I've written it down!

Good for me God I am broke;
Good that this famine made it worse.
Suffering made me think of You
And I vomited this world.

Good for me Lord my wife's a shrew;
Good that I'm stripped in public view.
I am blessed that the whole world insults me;
Thank you, I've lost all property.

How nice it feels to be without any shame!
What a relief! Now I'm all Yours.
Good that I rebuilt Your ruined shrine
Instead of salvaging my shattered home.

Says Tuka, I'm glad I fasted on your day
Starving has kept me stark awake.


## Pandharpur

The Great Ghost of Pandhari*
Pounces upon every one who passes by.

The forest is haunted by many spirits.
Whoever enters it finds it maddening.

O do not ever go there—you!
Nobody who goes in ever comes back.

Only once did Tuka go to Pandhari:
He hasn't been born ever since.


Who will help me to reason this out?
Who will raise my sagging morale?
I am no well-read philosopher or pundit,
I am just a casteless destitute.

* Pandhari: Place of pilgrimage that all worshippers of Vitthal want to visit once.

In this anarchic Age of Kali
The sharp ones will pounce on me for singing your praises.
I am in this tormenting double-bind:
To sing of You or not to sing.
Says Tuka, now that the people are all distanced from me,
Should I continue to be or end my being?


This whole transaction is a fraud.
I will have nothing more to do with you.

You do not operate under one name.
You have thousands of aliases.

When one tries to seek your true identity,
You begin to play hide and seek.

Says Tuka,
You are full of mischief.


In this Age of Evil poetry is an infidel's art:
The world teems with theatrical performers.

Their craving for money, lusting for women, and sheer
reproduction
Define their values and priorities:
And what they mouth has no connection with their own being.

Hypocrites! They pretend such concern for where the world is
going,
Talk of self-sacrifice, which is far from their minds.

They cite Vedic injunctions but can't do themselves any good.
They are unable to view their own bodies in perspective.

Says Tuka a torturesome death awaits
All those whose language is divorced from being.
Whirl around yourself

And the world
Seems to whirl
Around you

Stand still
And everything
Is stilled
Within a vast stillness

Yell
And echoes will ring
Says Tuka—
When clouds race
The moon seems to run


The absolutely naked
use their hands for a cup

When one really needs God
The mind presents Him

The alms one gets fulfil one's wishes
One sleeps in open spaces

Tuka is clothed by the sky itself
He lives beyond all perception

## Tukaram Says Farewell

See me off and go home now,
All of you.

May you attain the good by doing your duty righteously.
My blessings go with you.

You raised me and handed me over to the One.
Now everything will work out for me.

I have followed what I cherished:
It is time to go with the Lord of my breath.

Do not let your affection linger any longer:
Still your troubled minds.

Those who ever joined hands with me
have achieved man's cherished integrity.

Says Tuka, this is our last meeting;
All I leave behind is stories about me.

*—Translated by Dilip Chitre**

* Chitre, Dilip. 2003. *Says Tuka – 1: Selected Poems of Tukaram*. Pune: Sontheimer Cultural Association.

# NORTH

# Lal Ded

Almost certainly Lal Ded was born in the early 1300s in Kashmir, of Hindu parents. Her *vaakh* (verses, sayings), suggest an early education in her father's house and eventual marriage into a brahmin family of Pampor, where she was cruelly treated by her mother-in-law. She took to visiting the nearby river early each morning, crossing it to secretly worship Nata Keshava Bhairava, a form of Siva. Her mother-in-law suspected her of infidelity, rivers in Indian lore being invariably the site of clandestine trysts. One day, when she returned with a pot of water on her head, her husband in a fit of rage struck it with a staff. The crock shattered but the water remained 'frozen' in place until she had filled the household containers. The remaining water she tossed out the door where it formed a miraculous lake, said to exist in the early twentieth century, but dry today.

Word of her miracles spread. Crowds came to take darshan with her, violating her love of solitude, and at some point she left the house of her in-laws to take up the homeless life. Legend has it she wandered naked, singing and dancing in ecstasy like the 'Hebrew *nabi*s of old and the more modern Dervishes', as one muslim chronicler tells it. Muslim chronicles are full of her encounters with their holy men, and Hindu texts speak of gurus. It's likely she regarded Siddha Shrikantha, a Saivite, as her teacher, and one of her vaakh begins—

My guru gave a single precept:
draw your gaze from outside to inside
and fix on the inner self.
I, Lalla, took this to heart,
and naked set forth to dance

She became known as a Saivite yogini, and in her vaakh calls herself Lalla. Tales of her insight and magical powers outstripping those of her teachers circulated, though no records of her appear until centuries after her death. Even her death was a miraculous disappearance, when she dramatically climbed into an earthen pot, pulled another pot over herself, and vanished forever. In her day, Kashmir held Buddhists,

Nath yogins, Muslims, and brahmin teachers, all of whom may have influenced her. The likelihood, though, from her own songs, is that she remained devoted to *nila-kantha*, Siva, 'the blue-throated god'.

> Beneath you yawns a pit.
> How can you dance over it,
> how can you gather belongings?
> There's nothing you can take with you.
> How can you even
> savor food or drink?                                    (3)

> I have seen an educated man starve,
> a leaf blown off by bitter wind.
> Once I saw a thoughtless fool
> beat his cook.
> Lalla has been waiting
> for the allure of the world
> to fall away.                                           (9)

> Ocean and the mind are alike.
> Under the ocean
> flames *vadvagni*, the world-destroying fire.
> In man's heart twists the
> flame of rage.
> When that one bursts forth,
> its searing words of wrath and abuse
> scorch everything.
> If you weigh the words
> calmly, though, imperturbably,
> you'll see they have no substance,
> no weight.                                              (41)

> It provides your body clothes.
> It wards off the cold.
> It needs only scrub & water to survive.
> Who instructed you, O brahmin,

to cut this sheep's throat—
to placate a lifeless stone?                                    (65)


I might scatter the southern clouds,
drain the sea, or cure someone
hopelessly ill.
But to change the mind
of a fool
is beyond me.                                                  (19)


I came by the public road
but won't return on it.
On the embankment I stand, halfway
through the journey.
Day is gone. Night has fallen.
I dig in my pockets but can't find a
cowrie shell.
What can I pay for the ferry?                                  (5)


The god is stone.
The temple is stone.
Top to bottom everything's stone.
What are you praying to,
learned man?
Can you harmonize
your five bodily breaths
with the mind?                                                 (66)


You are the earth, the sky,
the air, the day, the night.
You are the grain
the sandalwood paste
the water, flowers, and all else.
What could I possibly bring
as an offering?                                                (70)

Solitary, I roamed the extent of Space,
leaving calculation behind.
The place of the hidden Self
opened and suddenly
out of the filth
bloomed a lotus.                                    (103)


O Blue-Throated God
I have the same six constituents* as you,
yet separate from you
I'm miserable.
Here's the difference—
you have mastered the six
I've been robbed by them.                           (128)


I, Lalla, entered
the gate of the mind's garden and saw
Siva united with Sakti.
I was immersed in the lake of undying bliss.
Here, in this lifetime,
I've been unchained from the wheel
of birth and death.
What can the world do to me?                        (130)

*—Revised from the translations by Jayalal Kaul†*

# Kabir

Modern scholars and popular tradition agree that Kabir was born in the
city of Varanasi in 1398 to a family of Muslim weavers. Few other details

---

* The six *kancukas*, 'husks' or 'coverings' of existence in Kashmir Saivism:
appearance, form, time, knowledge, passion, and fate.
† Kaul, Jayalal. 1973. *Lal Ded*. New Delhi: Sahitya Akademi.

of his life can be backed up by scholarly authority. An enormous body of legend has accrued around Kabir, most of the tales revealing a poet of uncompromising honesty, a singer so confrontational that he stands unique in history, and a man who displays a wily, trickster personality, a character that in North America would be called a 'coyote'. A figure of mischief, ruthlessly unpredictable, full of shivery ambiguity, Kabir has left in his wake a series of invaluable teachings, treasured by several different creeds. His admirers may sit at odds with one another, but they agree on Kabir's status.

Kabir's teacher is reputed to have been a celebrated Hindu yogin, Ramanand. The story goes that Kabir sought Ramanand out, intuiting that this man must be his teacher. But Ramanand would not accept Kabir as a student due to his Muslim origins. Not to be deterred, Kabir rose in the predawn dark one morning, and went down to the ghats of Varanasi where he knew Ramanand passed every day for his early ablutions and prayers. He lay on the steps directly in Ramanand's path. The yogin stumbled over Kabir in the pre-dawn darkness, and in surprise and fear blurted out his personal mantra, 'Ram! Ram!' On the basis of that, Kabir insisted Ramanand had transmitted the mantra and, therefore, by longstanding tradition had to accept Kabir as a student.

One of Kabir's *sakhi*s, or couplets, gets cited to support the belief that he was illiterate.

I don't touch ink or paper,
this hand never grasped a pen.
The greatness of the four ages
Kabir tells with his mouth alone.

Another sakhi suggests that his razor-toothed poems drew down hostility from both brahmins and Muslims, and adds to tales of his outspokenness.

If I speak out I'm beaten.
When the veil's up, no one sees.
The dog hides under the haystack.
Why talk and make enemies?

As with so many north Indian poets, Kabir's work comes to our period in two ways. First, it exists as oral poetry, sung in the streets, temples, bazaars, and fields, as well as on the concert hall stage. It also arrives as written texts. Three main literary traditions have conserved his poems: the Guru Granth of the Sikhs in the Punjab, the *Pancavani* of the Dadu Panth from Rajasthan, and the Kabir Panth of eastern India, for whom the *Bijak* is scripture. The French scholar Charlotte Vaudeville has distinguished a 'western tradition' of Kabir—those of the Sikhs and the Dadu Panth—from an eastern tradition. The eastern tradition, notably the poems of the *Bijak*, is fiercer, far more confrontational, and holds the uncompromising poetry that is nearly unique in its ferocity and inventiveness. Of the western Kabir, Linda Hess writes that it is, '… a softer, more emotional Kabir who sings of ecstatic insight, who experiences passionate longing for and tormented separation from a beloved, or who offers himself in utter surrender, as a servant or beggar, to a personified divine master. Often the western poet's expressions are coloured by the terms and forms of the Krishna *bhakti* movement.'

Miracles attended Kabir when alive, but little equals the story regarding his death. At his funeral, a group of Hindus and one of Muslims claimed him for their own. The Hindus insisted his remains be cremated, according to tradition. The Muslims argued for their own practice, burial. While Kabir's corpse lay under a shroud the two groups went from argument to blows. In the scuffle, the shroud was jolted back—and where Kabir's carcass once lay was a vast heap of flowers. The two groups divided the flowers, the Hindus burning theirs, the Muslims carting the other half off to bury.

Besides the eastern and western traditions of Kabir, there exists a third. This comes from a manuscript that emerged in Bengal in the nineteenth century and was translated into English by Rabindranath Tagore and Evelyn Underhill. The American poet Robert Bly later reworked Tagore's versions. This third Kabir, well known in North America—dubious as the contact with any 'authentic' Kabir might be—deserves recognition. It is, after all, the 'east meets west Kabir', having been influentially available in England and the United States for a hundred years.

## THE WESTERN TRADITION

The 'softer, more emotional' Kabir, preserved in books of both Sikhs and the Dadu Panth, has been well served by American poet Ezra

Pound, working from translations by Kali Mohan Ghose. Living in London, Pound knew Rabindranath Tagore—probably through William Butler Yeats who had composed the introduction to the British edition of *Gitanjali*. Through Tagore, Pound met the Bengali poetess Sarojini Naidu. One of them must have put him in contact with Ghose in 1912 or 1913. Pound already had an eye on Chinese and Japanese literature, though he was still a year or two away from the important poetic innovations of *Cathay* that would change English language poetry forever. Around the time he turned his attention to Kabir, he wrote his wife Dorothy, 'I seem to be getting orient from all quarters.'

Note the closeness of Pound's language to both Walt Whitman ('O opportune and well-omened!') and to the dignified erotic tenor of the Hebraic *Song of Songs*. Pound locates both a vocabulary and a cadence that feel deliberately archaic. Within that he has devised a measure that carries the stateliness, the bearing, of a classical raga singer on the concert hall stage. I have included all ten of his versions—originally published in *The Modern Review*, Calcutta, 1913—in order to recall how much the songs of Kabir, Mira, and Surdas have also come *off* the street, and made their way as part of high culture. Pound's versions stand in counterpoint to most translations of Kabir, which look to the eastern tradition, and try for the feel of a colloquial, quick-paced epigram.

Kabir's own verses are complicated by perplexing images, turns of phrase, and at times a baffling vocabulary. These figures are known as *ulatbamsi*, or 'upside down language'. Some of it may be initiatory, some deliberately paradoxical or irrational, much of it built on terms that might have sounded archaic or antiquated in Kabir's own day. With this in mind, Pound may have caught a strikingly accurate tone, with its cadences that sound a century or two out of date.

## From the English Versions of Kali Mohan Ghose

### I

The spring season is approaching,
Who will help me meeting with my dearest?

How shall I describe the beauty of the dearest,
Who is immersed in all beauties?
That color colors all the pictures of this universe,
Body and mind alike
Forget all things else in that beauty.
He who has these ideas,
The play of the spring is his.
This is the word which is unutterable.
Saith Kabir: There are very few who know this mystery.

## II

My beloved is awakened, how can I sleep?
Day and night he is calling me,
And instead of responding to his call
I am like an unchaste girl, living with another.
Saith Kabir: O clever confidant,
The meeting with the dearest is not possible without love.

## III

The scar aches day and night.
Sleep is not come.
Anxious for meeting with the dearest,
The father's house is not attractive at all.
The sky-gate opens,
The temple is manifested,
There now is the meeting with the husband.
I make oblation of my mind and body:
To the dearest the cup of the dearest!
Let flow the quick shower of rain from your eyes.
Cover your heart
With the intense deep blue
Assembling of the cloud.
Come near to the ear of the dearest,
Whisper to him your pain.
Saith Kabir: Here bring the meditation of the dearest,
Today's treasure of the heart.

## IV

It is true, I am mad with love. And what to me
Is carefulness or uncarefulness?
Who, dying, wandering in the wilderness,
Who is separated from the dearest?
My dearest is within me, what do I care?
The beloved is not asundered from me,
No, not for the veriest moment.
And I also am not asundered from him.
My love clings to him only,
Where is restlessness in me?
Oh my mind dances with joy,
Dances like a mad fool.
The raginis of love are being played day and night,
All are listening to that measure.
Rahu, the eclipse, Ketu, the Head of the Dragon,
And the nine planets are dancing,
And birth and death are dancing, mad with Ananda.
The mountain, the sea and the earth are dancing,
The Great Adornment is dancing with laughter and tears
     and smiles.
Why are you leaving 'the world',
You with the *tilak*-mark on your forehead?
While my mind is a-dancing through the thousand stages of
     its moon,
And the Lord of all his creation has found it acceptable dancing.

## V

O deserted bride,
How will you live in the absence of your beloved,
Without hunger in the day,
Sleepless in the night watches,
And every watch felt as if
It were the aeon of Kaliyuga?
The beautiful has deserted you in the full passion of his April.
Alas the fair is departed!

O Thou deserted,
Now begin to give up your house and your having.
Go forth to the lodge of the forest,
Begin to consider his name.
And if there he shall come upon you,
Then alone will you be come to your joy.
Eager as the caught fish for its water,
Be thou so eager to return!
Shapeless, formless and without line,
Who will be come to meet you,
O beautiful lady?
Take recognizance of your own wed Lord,
Behold him out of the center of your meditations,
Strip off the last of your errors,
And know that Love is your lord.
Saith Kabir: There is no second. Aeon
After aeon
Thou and I are the same.

## VI

Very difficult is the meeting with him,
How shall I be made one with my beloved?
After long consideration and after caution
I put my feet on the way, but every time
They have trembled and slipped aside.
The slippery path leads upward and the feet cannot hold
    to it.
The mind is taken in shyness,
For fear of the crowd
And out of respect to the family.
Oh where is my far beloved?
And I in the family dwelling!
And I can not escape my shyness!

## VII

How shall it be severed,
This love between thee and me?

Thou art lord, and I servant,
As the lotus is servant of water.
Thou art lord, and I servant,
As the Chakora is servant of the moonlight
And watches it all the night long.
The love between thee and me is from beginning to ending,
How can it end in time?
Saith Kabir: As the river is immersed in the ocean,
My mind is immersed in thee.

## VIII

Rishi Narad, that hast walked upon the winding path of the
    air,
That has walked there playing the Vina and singing thy
    song to Hari,
Rishi Narad, the beloved is not afar off,
I wake not, save in his waking,
I sleep not, save in his slumber.

## IX

O receiver of my heart,
Do thou come into my house,
My mind and body
Are but a pain, in thy absence.
When they say that I am your mistress
The shame of it is upon me.
If heart lie not upon heart,
How is the heart of love there?
The rice has no savor, the night is passed and is sleepless.
In the house and in the way of the forest my mind and
    thought have no rest.
Love-cup to the maid: water-cup to famished of thirst.
Is there one, bearer of fortune, to make clear my heart to
    my beloved?
Kabir is at the end of his patience
And dies without sight of his beloved.

## X

O bearer of love, give voice to the well-omened song.
The great lord is come to my house.
After employing my body in his love
I shall employ my mind.
The five mysteries will be enlightened with love.
The receiver of my heart, today is the guest in my house,
I am grown mad with my youth.
The pool of my body will be the place of pilgrimage.
Near by will Brahman chant Vedas,
The mind will be fused with my lover.

O opportune, and well-omened,
The three and thirty tunes of curious sound here with the
    sound of Ananda.
The paired lovers of the universe are assembled.
Saith Kabir: This day I set out for my marriage
With a bridegroom who is deathless.
In the quarter of my body there is music in process,
Thirty and six raginis are bound up into the burthen.
The bridegroom hath April play with me.
As Krishna with Radha, playing at the spring festival of
    Harilila,
I play at the spraying of colors, I and my beloved.
The whole universe is curious today.
Love and the rain of love are come hither with their showers.

—*Translated by Ezra Pound**

## THE EASTERN TRADITION

Much in Kabir is troublesome for listeners, readers, and translators,
particularly the expressions known as ulatbamsi, 'upside down language'
or reversed speech. These types of expression run throughout the *Bijak*,
and give the text its defining colour. Some of its nonsensical, irrational,
or veiled uses of speech may conceal initiatory secrets, making the

* Pound, Ezra. 1963. *Translations*. New York: New Directions.

poems ciphers that can only be opened fully by someone holding insider knowledge. Most of the poems require no key, however, for readers familiar with other irrational poetry—such as surrealism—and will be read for the states of mind they induce, rather than for logical argument.

In the eastern tradition dwells the Kabir who pins his listener with a walking dead man's eye, all his emotion built into a single objective—to shake you from deluded beliefs. The poems confront you as a listener, and offer no place to hide. Again and again they exhort reader or listener to shake off delusions, detach from transient desires, and to recognize how close death stands. The Ram of Kabir's poems often feels like a distant abstraction, as though only two powers exist. The first is death: 'Death waits in ambush.' The other, a thin, perilous possibility that through one's own abilities you can see through the lies and deceits: 'Whatever I say, nobody gets it. It's too simple.'

Three quotes by modern scholars:

Language trembled before him.

—H.P. Dvivedi

For sheer vigor of thought and rugged terseness of style, no later bhakti writer can be brought into comparison with him.

—W.G. Orr

His blunt language and rough words, his bitter irony, bespeak ardent indignation, but also a despearate effort to awaken his dumb, sleepy fellow men, who remain unaware of their impending doom.

—Charlotte Vaudeville

## Padas

When you die, what do you do with your body?
Once the breath stops
you have to put it away.
There are several ways to deal
with spoiled flesh.
Some burn it, some bury it
in the ground.

Hindus prefer cremation,
Turks burial.
But in the end, one way or another,
both have to leave home.
Death spreads the karmic net
like a fisherman snaring fish.
What is a man without Ram?
Kabir says, you'll be sorry later
when you go from this house
to that one.                                                    (61)

Saints, I see the world is mad.
If I tell the truth they rush to beat me,
if I lie they trust me.
I've seen the pious Hindus, rule-followers,
early morning bath-takers—
killing souls, they worship rocks.
They know nothing.
I've seen plenty of Muslim teachers, holy men
reading their holy books
and teaching their pupils techniques.
They know just as much.
And posturing yogis, hypocrites,
hearts crammed with pride,
praying to brass, to stones, reeling
with pride in their pilgrimage,
fixing their caps and their prayer-beads,
painting their brow-marks and arm-marks,
braying their hymns and their couplets,
reeling. They never heard of soul.
The Hindu says Ram is the Beloved,
the Turk says Rahim.
Then they kill each other.
No one knows the secret.
They buzz their mantras from house to house,
puffed with pride.
The pupils drown along with their gurus.

In the end they're sorry.
Kabir says, listen saints:
they're all deluded!
Whatever I say, nobody gets it.
It's too simple.                                    (4)


Hermit, that yogi is my guru
who can untie this song.
A tree stands without root,
without flowers bears fruit;
no leaf, no branch, and eight
sky-mouths thundering.
Dance done without feet,
tune played without hands,
praises sung without tongue,
singer without shape or form—
the true teacher reveals.
Seek the bird's, the fish's path.
Kabir says, both are hard.
I offer myself to an image:
the great being beyond boundaries
and beyond beyond.                                  (24)


Without Hari he's befuddled,
without a guru he's a mess.
Everywhere he goes
he loses himself
in nets within nets. The yogi says, 'Yoga's the top,
don't talk of seconds.'
Tuft of hair, shaven head, matted locks, vow of silence—
who's gotten anywhere?
Brainy ones, gifted ones,
heroes, poets, benefactors,
cry, 'I'm the greatest!'
They all go back where they came from
and don't take anything along.
Drop that wretched right hand and left

and grab Hari's feet—these very feet!
Kabir says, the dumb man has tasted sugar.
If you ask, what will he say?                                          (38)


Pandit, look in your heart for knowledge.
Tell me where untouchability
came from, since you believe in it.
Mix red juice, white juice and air—
a body bakes in a body.
As soon as the eight lotuses
are ready, it comes
into the world. Then what's
untouchable?
Eighty-four hundred thousand vessels
decay into dust, while the potter
keeps slapping clay
on the wheel, and with a touch
cuts each one off.
We eat by touching, we wash
by touching, from a touch
the world was born.
So who's untouched? asks Kabir.
Only she
who's free from delusion.                                             (41)


Lord!
A fire is raging
without fuel.
No one can put it out.
I know it spreads from you, enflaming
the whole world.
Even in water
the flames sprout.
Not one but nine streams
are burning. No one
knows any device.

As the city blazes, the watchman
sleeps happily, thinking,
'my house is secure.
Let the town burn, as long as my things
are saved.'
Ram, how your colours flicker!
In a hunchback's arms can a man's desires
be fulfilled?
Even as you think of this, you disappear
from birth to birth, your body forever
unsatisfied. No one is so stupid
as one who knows this
and pretends he doesn't.
Kabir asks, what's the way out
for such a fool?                                    (58)


The yogi's gone away
to a town of five women
in another country,
no one knows where.
He won't come back to his cave.
His rags are burnt, his flag torn,
his stick snapped, his bowl cracked.
Kabir says, This miserable Kaliyug!
What's in the pot
comes out the spout.                               (65)


No one knows the secret of the weaver
who spread his warp through the universe.
He dug two ditches, sky and earth,
made two spools, sun and moon,
filled his shuttle with a thousand threads,
and weaves till today: a difficult length!
Kabir says, they're joined by actions.
Good thread and bad,
that fellow weaves both.                           (28)

It's a heavy confusion.
Veda, Koran, holiness, hell, woman, man,
a clay pot shot with sperm ...
When the pot falls apart what do you call it?
Numskull! You've missed the point.
It's all one skin and bone, one piss and shit,
one blood, one meat.
From one drop, a universe.
Who's Brahmin? Who's Shudra?
Brahma *rajas*, Shiva *tamas*, Vishnu *sattva* ...
Kabir says, plunge into Ram!
There: No Hindu. No Turk.                                    (75)


It's not a wild beast, brother,
not a wild beast,
but everyone eats the meat.
The beast is a whole world—
unimaginable!
Tear open the belly,
no liver or guts.
It's this kind of meat, brother:
every minute sold.
Bones and hooves on the dump—
fire and smoke
won't eat it.
No head, no horn,
and where's a tail?
All the pandits meet
and fight.
Kabir sings a marriage song.                                 (88)


No one reads Vedas in the womb.
No Turk was born circumcised.
Dropped from the belly at birth,
a man puts on his costumes
and goes through his acts.
On that day you and I had one blood,

and one desire for life
engulfed us.
The world was born from one mother.
What wisdom teaches separation?
When you come from the vagina, you're a child.
When you enjoy the vagina,
they call you a man.
No one knows this ineffable movement—
how could one tongue describe it?
If any man has a million mouths and tongues,
let that great one speak.

Your life—from here
to there! shouts Kabir.
Without Ram's name, the worlds
into dying worlds
disappear.                                    (from R 1)

## Sakhis

Why is the doe thin
by the green
pool? One deer,
a hundred thousand
hunters. How to escape
the spear?                                     (18)


The three worlds are a cage,
virtue and vice a net.
Every creature is the prey,
and one hunter:
Death.                                         (19)

The road the pandits took,
crowds took.

Ram's pass is a high one.
Kabir keeps climbing.                                    (31)


Kabir's house is at the top
of a narrow, slippery track.
An ant's foot
won't fit.
So, villain,
why load your bullock?                                  (33)


Gorakh was yoga's connoisseur.
They didn't cremate
his body.
Still his meat rotted and mixed
with dust. For nothing
he polished his body.                                   (43)


Into the looking-glass cavern
the dog goes running.
Seeing his own reflection,
he dies barking.                                        (58)


In an iron boat
loaded with stones,
a bundle of poison on his head,
he wants to cross over.                                 (235)


A raft of tied-together snakes
in the world-ocean.
Let go, and you'll drown.
Grasp, and they'll bite your arm.                       (118)


Homage to the milk
that yields butter.
In half a couplet of Kabir's
the life
of the four Vedas.                                      (131)

Bones burn like wood,
hair burns like grass.
Kabir burns in the liquor of Ram
like cotton in a wood house.                          (174)


Birth, death, youth,
and the fourth stage,
old age.
The way cat watches mouse,
Death waits in ambush.                               (340)


In the wood where lions
don't tread
and birds don't fly,
Kabir ranges
in meditation.                                       (274)

*—Translated by Linda Hess and Shukdev Singh**

## A 'RECEIVED' KABIR

The following translations are the most distinct versions of a 'received' Kabir, that is a Kabir who cannot be pinned down with any historical accuracy. The Bengali scholar Kshitimohan Sen made a collection of Kabir padas from oral and written sources, publishing them in four volumes in 1910 at Santiniketan. Rabindranath Tagore and the American anthropologist Ruth Underhill used Sen's collection to produce a book of one hundred Kabir poems translated into English. While their hundred poems remain popular, coming in and out of print over the years, the turgid, neo-Victorian diction makes the book nearly unreadable to contemporary ears ('hopeless', writes John Hawley). Robert Bly, a renowned North American poet, reworked forty-four of the Tagore–Underhill versions. He did so without knowing the original language, and has created a Kabir much inflected by Sufism:

The caller calls in a loud voice to the Holy One at
    dusk,

* Hess, Linda and Shukdev Singh. 2002. *The Bijak of Kabir*. New Delhi: Oxford University Press.

or:

Rain pours down outside;
and inside I long for the Guest.

Bly's *The Kabir Book* appeared in 1977 in the United States and has been in print continuously, going through many editions. In 2004 he published an expanded edition, *Kabir: Ecstatic Poems*, with ten additional translations. The fact that the source poems may come largely from rural singers, early in the twentieth century, makes any connection to a historical Kabir difficult to establish.

Bly's versions have had enormous influence. His translations are the Kabir of North America.

Oh friend, I love you, think this over
    carefully! If you are in love,
then why are you asleep?

If you have found him,
give yourself to him, take him.

Why do you lose track of him again and again?

If you are about to fall into heavy sleep anyway,
why waste time smoothing the bed
and arranging the pillows?

Kabir will tell you the truth: this is what love is like:
suppose you have to cut your head off
and give it to someone else,
what difference would that make?                    (3)

I talk to my inner lover, and I say, why such
    rush?
We sense that there is some sort of spirit that loves
    birds and animals and the ants—
perhaps the same one who gave a radiance to you in
    your mother's womb.

Is it logical you would be walking around entirely
    orphaned now?
The truth is you turned away yourself,
and decided to go into the dark alone.
Now you are tangled up in others, and have forgotten
    what you once knew,
and that's why everything you do has some weird
    failure in it.                                                    (7)


Friend, hope for the Guest while you are alive.
Jump into experience while you are alive!
Think ... and think ... while you are alive.
What you call 'salvation' belongs to the time before
death.

If you don't break your ropes while you're alive,
do you think
ghosts will do it after?

The idea that the soul will join with the ecstatic
just because the body is rotten—
that is all fantasy.
What is found now is found then.
If you find nothing now,
you will simply end up with an apartment in the City
    of Death.
If you make love with the divine now, in the next life
    you will have the face of satisfied desire.

So plunge into the truth, find out who the Teacher is,
    believe in the Great Sound!

Kabir says this: When the Guest is being searched for,
    it is the intensity of the longing for the Guest that
    does all the work.
Look at me, and you will see a slave of that intensity.        (8)

The flute of interior time is played whether we
    hear it or not.
What we mean by 'love' is its sound, coming in.
When love hits the farthest edge of excess, it reaches
    wisdom.
And the fragrance of that knowledge!
It penetrates our thick bodies,
it goes through walls.
Its network of notes has a structure as if a million
    suns were arranged inside.
This tune has truth in it.
Where else have you heard a sound like this?                    (21)


Friend, wake up! Why do you go on sleeping?
The night is over—do you want to lose the day
    the same way?
Other women who managed to get up early have
    already found an elephant or a jewel ...
So much was lost already while you slept ...
and that was so unnecessary!

The one who loves you understood, but you did not.
You forgot to make a place in your bed next to you.
Instead you spent your life playing.
In your twenties you did not grow
because you did not know who your Lord was.
Wake up! Wake up! There's no one in your bed—
He left you during the night.
Kabir says: The only woman awake is the woman
    who has heard the flute!                              (29)


To whom shall I go to learn about the one I love?
Kabir says: 'When you're trying to find a hardwood forest,
    it seems wise to know what a tree is.
If you want to find the Lord, please forget about abstract
    nouns.'                                                 (40)

I played for ten years with girls my own age,
   but now I am suddenly in fear.
I am on the way up some stairs—they are high.
Yet I have to give up my fears
if I want to take part in this love.

I have to let go the protective clothes
and meet him with the whole length of my body.
My eyes will have to be the love-candles this time.
Kabir says: Men and women in love will understand
   this poem.
If what you feel for the Holy One is not desire,
then what's the use of dressing with such care,
and spending so much time making your eyelids
   dark?                                                         (41)


There is nothing but water in the holy pools.
I know, I have been swimming in them.
All the gods sculpted of wood or ivory can't say a word.
I know, I have been crying out to them.
The Sacred Books of the East are nothing but words.
I looked through their covers one day sideways.
What Kabir talks of is only what he has lived
   through.
If you have not lived through something, it is not
   true.                                                         (44)


I don't know what sort of a God we have been
   talking about.
The caller calls in a loud voice to the Holy One at
   dusk.
Why? Surely the Holy One is not deaf.
He hears the delicate anklets that ring on the feet of
   an insect as it walks.

Go over and over your beads, paint weird designs on
   your forehead,

wear your hair matted, long, and ostentatious,
but when deep inside you there is a loaded gun, how
can you have God?                                    (58)
                              —*Translated by Robert Bly**

# Ravidas (Raidas)

His birth date traditionally given as 1376 (some sources give 1398), raised on the outskirts of Varanasi, Ravidas would have been a contemporary of Kabir. He belonged to the group of untouchables known as *chamars*—leather workers, tanners, and cobblers—and his presence in the better districts or renowned temples of Varanasi would likely have been forbidden. Contact with dead animals has been regarded as an especially polluting activity in India, and the chamars, often shoe makers, have been said to be like the sole of a shoe at the bottom of the Hindu hierarchy. Ravidas's songs are explicit about his low social status, and equally articulate in declaring that only spiritual insight confers authentic status on anyone.

'A family that has a true follower of the Lord,' sang Ravidas in the face of brahminical prejudice, 'is neither high caste nor low caste.' Modern scholars point out that most families of bhakti saints or poets include members from the lowest castes, and Ravidas holds this position in north India. Some would regard his status as lower even than Kabir, the weaver from a Muslim family, due to Ravidas's contact with animal skin. Identifying himself with a far-ranging bhakta family, however, Ravidas finds his dignity among the poets, naming in his songs the fourteenth century Maharashtrian tailor, Namdev, another low-caste Marathi speaker, Trilocan, as well as Kabir. 'In mentioning these three as recipients of divine grace along with himself,' writes American scholar John Hawley, 'Ravidas underscored his sense of solidarity with a tradition of bhakti that flowed with particular animation in the lower ranks of society.'

* Bly, Robert. 2004. *Kabir: Ecstatic Poems.* Boston: Beacon Press.

Oral tradition, and written accounts that came later, tell of Ravidas meeting not only Kabir, but Mirabai, the Rajasthani princess, Gorakhnath, the guru of the Nath yogins, Ramanand, the legendary teacher of Kabir, and Nanak, the first Sikh guru. The *Adi Granth*, the most revered Sikh scripture, includes some of the earliest written poems of Ravidas.

Historically, one of the oldest strata of Ravidas's poetry are forty padas found in the *Adi Granth*, and a number of others held within scriptures of the Dadu Panth. There also exists a modern collection, gathered by a retired civil servant, B.R. Ghera, between 1963 and 1967. Ghera received his versions from a yogin and teacher named Harnam, who lived in a district east of Delhi. Ghera's ambition in compiling a large number of Ravidas songs was to produce a foundational anthology for the Adi Dharmis—a movement that traces its origins to a period prior to Aryan incursion into India. In particular, the Adi Dharma ('Original' Dharma) rejects the caste system as non-Indian.

But as John Hawley points out, the padas collected by B.R. Ghera use a language 'flatter and more plodding than one meets in the *Adi Granth*', and Hawley suggests that these poems, gathered in the 1960s from undocumented sources, are likely not very old. Yet so little historical fact attaches to Ravidas that we must largely credit a lengthy oral tradition with having forged the image held of him today. This tradition includes the accounts of his meeting with so many members of the north Indian family of bhaktas.

The following poems all come from the older Ravidas strata, being recorded in the *Adi Granth* (AG).

I've never known how to tan or sew,
    though people come to me for shoes.
I haven't the needle to make the holes
    or even the tool to cut the thread.
Others stitch and knot, and tie themselves in knots
    while I, who do not knot, break free.
I keep saying Ram and Ram, says Ravidas,
    and Death keeps his business to himself.       (AG 20)

A family that has a true follower of the Lord
Is neither high caste nor low caste, lordly or poor.

The world will know it by its fragrance.
Priests or merchants, laborers or warriors,
  halfbreeds, outcastes, and those who tend cremation fires—
    their hearts are all the same.
He who becomes pure through love of the Lord
  exalts himself and his family as well.
Thanks be to his village, thanks to his home,
  thanks to that pure family, each and every one,
For he's drunk with the essence of the liquid of life,
  and he pours away all the poisons.
No one equals someone so pure and devoted—
  not priests, not heroes, not parasolled kings.
As the lotus leaf floats above the water, Ravidas says,
  so he flowers above the world of his birth.          (AG 29)


Mother, she asks, with what can I worship?
  All the pure is impure. Can I offer milk?
The calf has dirtied it sucking its mothers teat.
  Water, the fish have muddied; flowers, the bees—
No other flowers could be offered than these—
  The sandalwood tree, where the snake has coiled, is spoiled.
The same act formed both nectar and poison.
  Everything's tainted—candles, incense, rice—
But still I can worship with my body and my mind
  and I have the guru's grace to find the formless lord.
Rituals and offerings—I can't do any of these.
  What, says Ravidas, will you do with me?          (AG 13)


The walls are made of water, pillared by air,
  sealed together with the mortar of blood,
A cell of veins and meat and bones,
  a cage to hold this poor bird.
Who cares what is yours or mine?—
  for we nest in this tree only briefly.
As high as you can build, as low as you can dig,
  your size will never swell the dimensions of a grave;
Those lovely curls, that turban tied so rakishly—

they'll soon be turned to ash.
If you've counted on the beauty of your wife and home
   without the name of Ram, you've already lost the game.
And me: even though my birth is mean,
   my ancestry by everyone despised,
I have always trusted in you, King Ram,
   says Ravidas, a tanner of hides.             (AG 19)


It's just a clay puppet, but how it can dance!
It looks here, looks there, listens and talks,
   races off this way and that;
It comes on something and it swells with pride,
   but if fortune fades it starts to cry.
It gets tangled in its lusts, in tastes
   of mind, word, and deed,
      and then it meets its end and takes some other form.
Brother, says Ravidas, the world's a game, a magic show,
   and I'm in love with the gamester,
      the magician who makes it go.          (AG 12)


The house is large, its kitchen vast,
   but after only a moment's passed, it's vacant.
This body is like a scaffold made of grass:
   the flames will consume it and render it dust.
Even your family—your brothers and friends—
   clamor to have you removed at dawn.
The lady of the house, who once clung to your chest,
   shouts 'Ghost! Ghost!' now and runs away.
The world, says Ravidas, loots and plunders all—
   except for me, for I have slipped away
      by saying the name of God.          (AG 27)


The day it comes, it goes;
   whatever you do, nothing stays firm.
The group goes, and I go;
   the going is long, and death is overhead.
What! Are you sleeping? Wake up, fool,

wake to the world you took to be true.
The one who gave you life daily feeds you, clothes you;
   inside your body, he runs the store.
So keep to your prayers, abandon 'me' and 'mine',
   now's the time to nurture the name that's in the heart.
Life has slipped away. No one's left on the road,
   and in each direction the evening dark has come.
Madman, says Ravidas, here's the cause of it all—
   it's only a house of tricks. Ignore the world.          (AG 26)

*—Translated by John Hawley and Mark Juergensmeyer**

# Surdas

Surdas is the renowned blind bhakti poet of north India. Along with
Mirabai, he remains one of the most commonly presented by classical
singers on the concert hall stage. An enormous corpus of songs attributed
to him—amounting to four or five thousand but legendarily numbered
at 1,25,000 padas—are collectively titled the *Sur Sagar*, the 'Ocean
of Sur'. Reliable facts about Surdas's life have been long veiled by a
sectarian hagiography, recorded in the *Caurasi Vaisnavan ki Varta*, or
'Conversations with Eighty-four Vaishnavas', attributed to Gokulnath,
whose traditional birthdate of 1551 suggests that as a young man he
might conceivably have met an elderly Surdas.

   The *Varta* and its commentary place Surdas in the lineage of
Vallabhacharya, founder of a devotional community, the Vallabha
Sampraday, and make Vallabha his guru, the one who wakened him
from spiritual torment. Yet Sur's translator, John Hawley, writes:

There is good reason to believe that sectarianism has left a deep mark on the
biography of Sur. One of the main objectives in the *Varta*'s account of Sur's
life is to show how Sur became a pupil of Vallabha and then subsequently of
his son Vitthalnath, who assumed the leadership of the community when his

   * Hawley, John Stratton and Mark Juergensmeyer. 1988. *Songs of the Saints of
India*. New York: Oxford University Press.

father died. The reader is told in many ways what a profound effect this spiritual parentage had on Sur. Yet it is plain to the outsider's eye that the *Varta*'s effort to fashion Sur's poetry in the image of his supposed masters are but precious fabrications designed to cover up the fact that nowhere in the massive collection of verse attributed to Sur ... is mention made of Vallabha or the theology of his sect.

Stories abound concerning Sur's miserable childhood, his blindness, his poverty, and his unsympathetic parents. The *Varta* and innumerable popular accounts regard him as blind from birth—and they date his first awakening to the age of six, when Sur heard a group of bhakti singers pass by his house. Scholars Kenneth Bryant and John Hawley have sifted out a group of 400 poems, from the ones signed with his name, that might authentically be linked to a historical Surdas. Little in those songs appears to substantiate a life of blindness, however. Hawley notes that the standard verses mustered as evidence could simply be complaints about the indignities of old age. The name, or more properly, the title, Surdas, has come to be used as a respectful address to a blind man, especially blind singers, who are met all over India today.

As with Mirabai, whose life overlaps with Surdas's, clearly what survives in written record and in popular culture cannot be the work of a single author. We would do better to refer to a Surdas tradition, added onto by dozens or even hundreds of singers from the sixteenth century until recent times.

One account of Surdas, depicted in paintings, posters, and other visual media, has him meeting with Emperor Akbar, who reputedly had a near obsession with Surdas's songs. Mirabai too is supposed to have met Akbar, but no historical records document either of these encounters. 'With Sur even the geography is unclear,' writes John Hawley, observing that the accounts of Surdas dwelling in Braj could simply be drawn from his poems, so many of which detail episodes from Krishna's life there.

Gopal has slipped in and stolen my heart, friend.
He stole through my eyes and invaded my breast
    simply by looking—who knows how he did it?—
Even though parents and husband and all
    crowded the courtyard and filled my world.
The door was protected by all that was proper;

not a corner, nothing, was left without a guard.
Decency, prudence, respect for the family—
    these three were locks and I hid the keys.
The sturdiest doors were my eyelid gates—
    to enter through them was a passage impossible—
And secure in my heart, a mountainous treasure:
    insight, intelligence, fortitude, wit.
And then, says Sur, he'd stolen it—
    with a thought and a laugh and a look—
        and my body was scorched with remorse.        (NPS 2490)

Thoughts of him stalk me, even in my dreams,
Now that he has gone; and oh, my friend, it hurts
    as hard as on the day that Nandanandan left.
Last night, in fact, that cowherd came to my house:
    he laughed his laugh and grasped me by the arm.
What am I to do? The night is now my foe.
    Will I ever know another wink of sleep?
I've become like a sheldrake who sees her own reflection,
    takes it as the gladdening image of her mate,
And then, says Sur, that menacing Creator
    masquerades as wind and brings ripples to the lake.   (NPS 3886)

Away! Go back to where you spent the night!
Manmohan, what clues are you trying to erase?
    Signs of tight embraces are not so quickly hid.
A necklace, now stringless, is etched into your chest:
    what clever girl was pressed against your sleeping heart?
Her hair is on your clothes, and your jewels are askew:
    they were tangled in a bout with her lust-hardened breasts.
Teethmarks, nailmarks: oh what you've endured
    to have your fill of passion in that other woman's lair.
Surdas says, your honey lips have lost their sheen
    and your sleepless eyes bear the weight of lethargy.   (NPS 3122)

Ever since your name has entered Hari's ear
It's been 'Radha, oh Radha', an infinite mantra,

a formula chanted to a secret string of beads.
Nightly he sits by the Jumna, in a grove
    far from his friends and his happiness and home.
He yearns for you. He has turned into a yogi:
    constantly wakeful, whatever the hour.
Sometimes he spreads himself a bed of tender leaves;
    sometimes he recites your treasurehouse of fames;
Sometimes he pledges silence: he closes his eyes
    and meditates on every pleasure of your frame—
His eyes the invocation, his heart the oblation,
    his mutterings the food to feed
        the priests who tend the fire.
So has Syam's whole body wasted away.
    Says Sur, let him see you. Fulfill his desire.          (NPS 3399)


I, only I, am best at being worst, Lord.
It's me! The others are powerless to match me.
    I set the pace, forging onward, alone.
All those others are a flock of amateurs,
    but I have practiced every day since birth,
And look: you've abandoned me, rescuing the rest!
    How can I cause life's stabbing pain to cease?
You've favored the vulture, the hunter, tyrant, whore,
    and cast me aside, the most worthless of them all.
Quick, save me, says Sur, I'm dying of shame:
    who ever was finer at failure than I?          (NPS 138)


Life has stumbled, stumbled, unraveled,
Roped to politics and salary and sons.
    Without my even noticing, my life has ambled off
And gotten tangled in a snare of illusion so foolproof
    that now I cannot break it or loosen its grip.
Songs of the Lord, gatherings of the good—
    I left myself hanging in air without either
Like an overeager acrobat who does just one more trick
    because he cannot bear to close the show.

What splendor, says Sur, can you find in flaunting wealth
   when your husband, your lover, has gone?       (NPS 292)

Now I am blind; I've shunned Hari's name.
My hair has turned white with illusions and delusions
   that have wrung me through till nothing makes sense.
Skin shriveled, posture bent, teeth gone;
   my eyes emit a stream of tears;
      my friends, a stream of blame.
Those eyes once ranged as free as a cat's,
   but failed to measure the play of Time
Like a false-eyed scarecrow failing to scatter
   the deer from the field of the mind.
Surdas says, to carry on without a song for God
   is courting Death: his club stands poised
      above your waiting head.       (Jodhpur 1359/14)

Until you wake up to what you really are
You'll be like the man who searches the whole jungle
   for a jewel that hangs at his throat.
Oil, wick, and fire: until they mingle in a cruse
   they scarcely produce any light.
So how can you expect to dissipate the darkness
   simply by talking about lamps?
You're the sort of fool who sees your face
   in a mirror, befouled by inky filth,
And proceeds to try to erase the blackness
   by cleaning the reflection to a shine.
Surdas says, it's only now the mind can see—
   now that so many countless days are lost and gone—
For who has ever recognized the brilliance of the sun
   but by seeing it through eyes gone blind?      (NPS 368)

       —*Translated by John Hawley and Mark Juergensmeyer**

---

\* Hawley, John Stratton and Mark Juergensmeyer. 1988. *Songs of the Saints of India*. New York: Oxford University Press.

# Mirabai

Of the poets of medieval India, Mirabai is the one who has most fired the imagination of India over the centuries. Her songs, originally thought to be in a Rajasthani–Gujarati dialect, have moved across linguistic boundaries easily, and people sing them not just across the north but into the deep subcontinent south as well. One of the most highly regarded and best-selling recordings in India's history was a volume of Mira bhajans sung by M.S. Subbulakshmi, herself a native of the south. At least ten feature-length films have been made based on the story of Mirabai, in one of which Subbulakshmi played the title role. Mira has meanwhile been sung repeatedly by classical purists like Kishori Amonkar, and by popular artists like Anuradha Paudwal.

The original account of Mirabai's life comes from the *Bhaktamala* of Nabhadas, an account of the northern bhakti saints composed around 1600 CE.

Mira shattered the manacles
of civility, family, and shame.
A latter day *gopi*, she made love explicit
for the dark Kali Yuga.
Independent, unutterably fearless,
she sang her delight for an
amorous god.
Scoundrels considered her treacherous
and ventured to kill her,
but draining like nectar the poison they sent
she came forth unscathed.
Striking the drumskin of worship
Mira cringed before no one.
Family, civility, gossip—
she shattered the manacles.
She sang praise to her lord Giridhara.

This account holds the skeletal version of what has passed for Mirabai's story. She was born into a Rajput family in the town of Merta, in Rajasthan. As a young girl she once met a sadhu at the door to her family palace, and he slipped into her fist a tiny icon of Krisna Giridhara, 'lifter of the mountain'. In that form, Krishna is depicted pressing Mt. Govardhan like an umbrella over his head, to shield the cattle and cowherds of Braj from the wrath of the old Vedic chieftain-god Indra. Indra is angrily pelting the people of the region with thunderbolts and rain for having neglected his puja. Besides giving Mirabai the image, this mysterious sadhu—who never gets named—may have whispered into Mira's ear 'a true word', a phrase that appears in several songs from the Mirabai canon. From that moment, it is said, Mira conceived not only an impossibly deep hunger for Krishna, but never wavered in her belief that he had been pledged to her in marriage.

Married by her parents at a young age into a neighbouring clan, possibly as part of a military alliance, Mirabai infuriated her in-laws. On the day of her wedding, brought home in a royal palanquin, she ignored the traditional gesture of bowing to her mother-in-law's feet when she entered the house. Then she refused to acknowledge the goddess image the family held in esteem. It is possible her husband was weak-minded, and some accounts say he perished on the field of battle shortly after their marriage. All the stories agree, though, that Mira had refused to sleep with him, claiming her true husband was Shyam, the 'Dark One', the name she used for her true love and lord.

Her family—her husband's family, that is—was humiliated and outraged. The *Rana*, as she refers to him in her songs (who may have been a brother-in-law), made three attempts on her life, aided by the spurned mother-in-law. First they sent her a poisoned fluid, claiming it to be *charanamrita*—water that, having been used to wash the feet of a Krishna image, had turned to *amrita*. Mira drained the lethal brew and 'came forth unscathed'.

A second attempt to murder her—with a serpent concealed in a basket of fruit—also failed. When Mira lifted the lid, the asp became a *saligram*, a black fossil ammonite identified as an image of Krishna. After a third attempt on her life, Mira fled her in-law's palace or fortress, and took to the streets. All along she had insisted her true family was the *sadhu sang*, or company of truth seekers, and now she ran from her life of privilege—a privilege that weighed upon her like chains. For the rest of her life she moved among the family of bhaktas.

Mirabai's songs are a mystery. No authenticated manuscripts survive from within two centuries of her death. One legend says she sang her songs as she travelled, and a loyal maid named Lalita, who had abandoned the palace to join her on the roads of north India, transcribed the songs into a great notebook. This notebook has not been seen for centuries. Modern collectors have located well over 5,000 songs attributed to her, and several scholars have attempted to determine an original corpus, based on linguistic evidence. Western critics seem sceptical that any of the songs can be termed authentic, and a prevalent view in the west is that a historical Mirabai simply cannot be affirmed. She may be legendary, and the songs the creation of a lengthy tradition of singers composing with a set of techniques or out of a particular state of belief, using the name Mirabai as their signature.

Yet there is the troubling fact of the stories that surround some central figure named Mirabai. And there remains the more deeply troubling fact of a vast number of songs so consistent in form, so vivid in their yearning for her Dark Lord, so subversive of social institutions like marriage, and so troubling for religious propriety. More than that, her songs carry a personal flair, combined of yearning, risk, anguish, and dignity, that feel more personal and vivid than those of any other singer of north India. It is also worth observing that her songs verge close to folk metres, using a simpler language and more repetition than the verse of other renowned north Indian bhakti poets. Could the songs have survived orally for centuries, possibly among women, without getting transcribed?

One final story. Mira ended up at the great temple in Dwarka, having left the Vrindavan region associated with most of her wanderings. Her husband's family after many years decided they wanted her home—possibly on account of her fame, and because of a persistent local rumour that they had suffered a series of military setbacks as a kind of karmic reaction to their poor treatment of Mira. They sent an envoy of brahmins to Dwarka to fetch her. When Mira refused to return with their envoy, the brahmins pressured her by vowing to fast to death if she wouldn't relent. Reluctantly she agreed to their demands, then requested a final night alone in the temple with her god. In the morning the envoy forced open the temple doors and found only Mira's hair and her robe, slung across the lap of the deity. Most accounts declare that like Antal 500

years earlier, she had been absorbed into her beloved. A more skeptical
modern commentator wonders if she might not have escaped out the
back door into the bay, and slipped off across the water.

Binding my ankles with silver
I danced—
people in town called me crazy.
She'll ruin the clan
said my mother-in-law,
and the prince
had a cup of venom delivered.
I laughed as I drank it.
Can't they see?
Body and mind aren't something to lose,
the Dark One's already seized them.
Mira's lord can lift mountains,
he is her refuge.

Sister, the Dark One won't speak to me.
Why does this useless body keep breathing?
Another night gone
and no one's lifted my gown.
He won't speak to me.
Years pass, not a gesture.
They told me
he'd come when the rains came,
but lightning pierces the clouds,
the clock ticks until daybreak
and I feel the old dread.
Slave to the Dark One,
Mira's whole life is a long
night of craving.

He has stained me,
the color of raven he's stained me.
Beating a clay

two-headed drum at both ends
like a nautch girl I dance
before sadhus.
Back in town I'm called crazy,
drunkard, a love slut—
they incited the prince
who ordered me poisoned
but I drained the cup without missing a step.
Mira's lord is the true prince,
he stained her the color of raven,
birth after birth
she is his.

O Mind,
praise the lotus feet that don't perish!
Consider all things
on heaven and earth—and their doom.
Go off with pilgrims, undertake fasts,
wrangle for wisdom,
trek to Banaras to die,
what's the use?
Arrogant body just withers,
phenomenal world is a coy parakeet
that flies off at dusk.
Why throw a hermit robe over your shoulders—
yellow rag yogins
are also bewildered,
caught every time in the birth snare.
Dark One, take this girl for your servant.
Then cut the cords and
set her free.

Yogin, don't go—
at your feet a slave girl has fallen.
She lost herself
on the devious path of romance and worship,

no one to guide her.
Now she's built
an incense and sandalwood pyre
and begs you to light it.
Dark One, don't go—
when only cinder remains
rub my ash over your body.
Mira asks, Dark One,
　　can flame twist upon flame?

Clouds—
I watched as they ruptured,
ash black and pallid I saw mountainous clouds
split and spew rain
for two hours.
Everywhere water, plants and rainwater,
a riot of green on the earth.
My lover's gone off
to some foreign country,
sopping wet at our doorway
I watch the clouds rupture.
Mira says, nothing can harm him.
This passion has yet
to be slaked.

You pressed Mira's seal of love
then walked out.
Unable to see you
she's hopeless,
tossing in bed—gasping her life out.
Dark One, it's your fault—
I'll join the yoginis,
I'll take a blade to my throat in Banaras.
Mira gave herself to you,
you touched her intimate seal
and then left.

Remember our pledge,
that you'd come to my cottage?
I'm strung out,
I stare down the road
and strain for a glimpse of you.
The hour we set
came and departed.
I sent a messenger girl
but Dark One, you tossed out the message
and deflowered the girl.
Days I don't see you are torment,
Mira knows you're with
somebody else.

How bitter is carnival day
with my lover off traveling.
O desolate town,
night and day wretched,
my small bed in the attic lies empty.
Rejected and lost
in his absence, stumbling under
the pain.
Must you wander
from country to country?  It hurts me.
These fingers ache
counting the days you've been gone.
Spring arrives
with its festival games,
the chiming of anklets, drumbeats and flute, a sitar—
yet no beloved visits my gate.
What makes you forget?
Here I stand begging you, Dark One
don't shame me!
Mira comes to embrace you
birth after birth
    still a virgin.

In my dream, sister,
the Lord of the Downtrodden wed me.
Deities danced in attendance,
fifty-six million,
the Dark One was groom in my dream.
In my dream were arched marriage gateways,
a clasping of hands, sister.
In a dream
the Lord of the Downtrodden
married Mira and took her to bed.
Good fortune from previous births
comes to fruit.

The plums tasted
sweet to the unlettered desert-tribe girl,
but what manners! To chew into each!
She was ungainly,
low-caste, ill mannered and dirty,
but the god took the
fruit she'd been sucking.
Why? She knew how to love.
She might not distinguish
splendor from filth
but she'd tasted the nectar of passion.
Might not know any Veda,
but a chariot swept her away.
Now she frolics in heaven, passionately bound to her god.
The Lord of Fallen Fools, says Mira,
will save anyone
who can practice rapture like that.
I myself in a previous birth
was a cow-herding girl
at Gokul.

Over the trees
a crescent moon glides.
The Dark One has gone to dwell in Mathura.

Me, I struggle, caught in a love noose
and yes,
Mira's lord can lift mountains
but today his passion
    seems distant and faint.


Listen, friend,
the Dark One laughs
and scours my body with ravenous eyes.
Eyebrows are bows,
darting glances are arrows that pierce
    a wrecked heart.

*You will heal*
*I'll bind you with magical diagrams*
*and crush drugs*
*for a poultice.*
*But if it's love that afflicts you*
    *my powers are worthless*

Sister, how can I heal?
I've already
crushed sandalwood paste,
tried witchcraft—charms and weird spells.
Wherever I go
his sweet form is laughing inside me.
Tear open these breasts
You'll see a torn heart!
Unless she sees her dark lover
how can Mira
    endure her own body?


This infamy, O my Prince,
is delicious!
Some revile me,
others applaud,

I simply follow my incomprehensible road.
A razor thin path
but you meet some good people,
a terrible path but you hear a true word.
Turn back?
Because the wretched stare and see nothing?
O Mira's lord is noble and dark,
and slanderers
rake only themselves
   over the coals.


Dark One,
how can I sleep?
Since you left my bed
the seconds drag past like epochs,
each moment
a new torrent of pain.  –
I am no wife,
no lover comes through the darkness—
lamps, houses, no comfort.
On my couch
the embroidered flowers
pierce me like thistles,
   I toss through the night.


Yet who would believe my story?
That a lover
bit my hand like a snake,
and the venom bursts through
   and I'm dying?


I hear
the peacock's faraway gospel,
the nightingale's love song,
the cuckoo—
thickness on thickness folds through the sky,

clouds flash with rain.
Dark One, is there no love
in this world
that such anguish continues?
Mirabai waits for a
    glance from your eye.


The Dark One's love-stain
is on her,
other ornaments
Mira sees as mere glitter.
A mark on her forehead,
a bracelet, some prayer beads,
beyond that she wears only
    her conduct.


Make-up is worthless
when you've gotten truth from a teacher.
O the Dark One has
stained me with love,
and for that some revile me,
others give honor.
I simply wander the road of the sadhus
    lost in my songs.


Never stealing,
injuring no one,
who can discredit me?
Do you think I'd step down from an elephant
to ride on the haunch
    of an ass?


Sister,
I went into market
and picked up the Dark One.

You whisper
as though it were shameful,
I strike my drum and declare it in public.
You say I paid high,
I say I weighed it out on the scales,
it was cheap.
Money's no good here,
I traded my body, I paid with my life!
Dark One, give Mira a glance,
we struck a bargain
    lifetimes ago.


Drunk, turbulent clouds
roll overhead
but they bring from the Dark One
no message.
Listen!
the cry of a peacock,
a nightingale's faraway ballad,
a cuckoo!
Lightning
flares in the darkness,
a rejected girl shivers,
thunder, sweet wind and rain.
Lifetimes ago
Mira's heart went with the Dark One,
tonight in her solitude
infidelity spits
    like a snake

*—Translated by Andrew Schelling**

* Schelling, Andrew. 1993. *For Love of the Dark One; Songs of Mirabai*. Illustrated by Mayumi Oda. Boston: Shambhala Publications (reprinted by Hohm Press, Prescott, 1998).

# Tulsidas

Tulsidas is one of India's most renowned poets today, celebrated for his retelling of the Ramayana in the Avadhi dialect of medieval Hindi, entitled *Ramacharitamanasa*, or 'The Holy Lake of Rama's Deeds'. Contemporary editions of the book often provide a modern Hindi version of his explicitly religious text. Huge crowds attend performances of the story of Rama—performances based on Tulsidas's text—during the week-long public festivals known as Ramalilas, held annually in towns across north India, with Varanasi providing the largest and most extravagant.

His birthplace traditionally given as Rajapur in modern-day Uttar Pradesh, Tulsidas is said to have been born in 1532, which would place his early life during the reign of Humayun. Twenty-two works are attributed to him, composed in either Sanskrit or Hindi. Because texts dating back to his lifetime survive—and he was indisputably a *writer* as well as a singer—contemporary scholars largely agree on what he wrote, so his oeuvre is free of the uncertainty surrounding the songs of his fellow northern Indian poets.

Yet the facts of Tulsidas's life are scant, despite a reputation that was secured during his own lifetime, and the stories are as fantastic as those of any other bhakti poet. Many first appear in Priyadas's commentary on the *Bhaktamal*. Accounts of a difficult childhood, affected by poverty and perhaps local plague, seem substantiated in Tulsi's poetry. Late in his life, while he was dwelling in Varanasi, Siva's city, disease again swept through. Tulsi attributes the scourge to a lethal conjunction of Saturn with the constellation Pisces, then suggests the cause to be some inexplicable grudge Siva held for the city. He insists the name of 'Rama' constitutes the only protection against childhood hardships and sweeping plagues, and the solitary path to salvation.

Early in his career as a poet—one widespread story has it—he loved his wife so desperately, or felt so insecure in his passion, that when he returned home from a journey and discovered she'd gone to her parents' house, he went nearly insane. A river swollen by rain separated him from his beloved wife, and he crossed it by commandeering a corpse for a raft. Reaching the house of his wife's parents, he drew himself up to her bedroom, mistaking a snake for a rope. His wife, appalled at the passion with which he'd clawed his way to her, greeted him with, 'If you felt for Lord Rama half the ardour you show for my body—bones covered with dirty skin—you would cross the ocean of *samsara* and know eternal bliss.' Stunned into a recognition of the futility of earthly love, Tulsi is said to have renounced family life, and left for Varanasi to take up a life of austere devotion.

Troublingly, Tulsidas is often cited for his accounts of the spiritual, ethical, and social collapses taking place in the Kali Yuga. He seems a staunch defender of the status quo, with the 'notorious claim', as David Lorenzen calls it, that 'shudras, fools, drums, cattle and women are all eligible for a beating'. Moreover, in Tulsi's view, one of the Kali Yuga's worst ills is that shudras and untouchables presume to the religious calling of the brahmins—a prejudice that sharply contrasts with the views of so many bhakti poets.

Composing his greatest work in Hindi, rather than the Sanskrit he was trained in, complicates Tulsidas's work. On the surface, little in his poetry should cause orthodox brahmins much perplexity—except for the irrevocable fact that Tulsi composed it not in the sacred Sanskrit language, but in a vernacular meant for commoners. Moreover, many of his stanzas—and many of the stories he himself recounts—erase the distinction between saguna and nirguna forms of devotion. Or more specifically, reconcile the two. Within the mysterious, illogical saguna sphere, where the divine has incarnated himself on earth, Siva, Rama, and Krishna, each receive their due, along with many other deities in the Hindu pantheon. In the end, though, it is the mysterious 'Ram' that alone provides consolation and wisdom.

> Say Ram, say Ram, say Ram,
>     you fool!
> That name is your raft
>     on the awful sea of life.
>
> It is the only way of gaining
>     true gain and wealth.
> For this sick age has swallowed ways
>     that helped in ages past.

Whether good or bad,
   right-handed or left,
In the end the name of Ram
   works for everyone.

This world is a sky garden
   of flowers and fruits,
Towers that are only clouds—
   you should never forget.

Those who abandon Ram's name
   for something else, Tulsi says,
leave the table set at home
   to beg for filthy scraps.


Madhav, you'll find none duller than I.
The moth and the fish, though lacking in wit,
   can scarcely approach my slow standard.
Transfixed by the shimmering shapes they meet,
   they fail to discern the dangers of fire and hook,
But I, who can see the perils of fiery flesh
   and still refuse to leave it, have wisdom even less.
I've drifted along in the grand and entrancing
   river of ignorance, a stream that knows no shores,
And abandoned the rescue raft of Hari's lotus feet
   to grasp after bubbles and foam
Like a dog so hungry that he lunges for a bone
   grown ancient and marrowless; and bitten so tight,
The bone scrapes his mouth and draws blood—
   his own blood—yet he tastes it with delight.
I too am trapped in jaws. The grip that clamps
   is that of a merciless snake, this life,
And I yearn for relief, a frightened frog, but have spurned
   the one chance I had: the bird that Hari rides.
Here and there other water creatures float;
   we are snared together in a tightening net:
Watch them, how greedily they feed on one another,

and they never sense that next may be their turn.
The goddess of learning could count my sins
    for countless ages, and still not be done,
Yet Tulsidas places his trust in the One
    who rescues the destitute, and in trusting hopes to live.


It's as if you thought your body
    was shielded with copper
        and you didn't need the Lord,
But don't you know, lowly one,
    that death is overhead?
Who hasn't surrounded himself
    with land and house,
Wife and wealth,
    sons and friends—
But whose have they become?
    Can they go with you when you go?
They are reflections
    of your own deceit, those loves.
Kings who conquered the world,
    who bound up the ruler of the realm of death—
Those great kings: Death ate them for breakfast.
    What, then, will he do with you?
Look, and think about what is true,
    what the Vedas themselves have sung;
Even now, Tulsi, though you know,
    you fail to praise the One
        on whom even Siva has set his mind.


This darkest of ages has destroyed
    the lines of caste, the stages of life:
All that is proper has been tossed aside
    like a bundle thrown to the ground.

Siva is angry:
    his anger is seen in the plague.

The Master is angry:
   daily poverty doubles.

They cry out, destitute men
   and women. No one hears.
Who are the gods who conspired to strike us
   with this thick, black-magic curse?

And then merciful Ram, remembered
   as protector of the terrified by Tulsi,
Praised for his fine compassion,
   gestured
      —he waved it all away.

                              —*Translated by John Hawley and Mark Juergensmeyer**

# Dadu Dayal

Dadu, often called Dadu Dayal or 'Dadu the Compassionate', was born
in Ahmedabad, around 1544, the adopted child of a low-caste merchant
and his wife. One account has it that his foster-father found him adrift
in a river and brought him home—a story that gathers around Kabir
as well, and probably represents a later effort to depict him as born to
a higher caste, brought up by low-caste foster parents. Dadu's disciples
spoke of him as a *dhuniya* or *pinjari*, that is, a cotton-carder, a profession
in which low-caste Hindus and Muslims lived closely together.

At age eleven Dadu had a vision of god, who appeared to him as an
aged, bearded man. This figure blessed Dadu before abruptly vanishing.
Again, at the age of eighteen, Dadu had another vision of the old man;
this one prompted him to leave home and follow the road as a wandering
ascetic. Eventually, he settled in the town of Sambhar and raised a
family. There he incurred the wrath of both Hindus and Muslims for

* Hawley, John Stratton and Mark Juergensmeyer. 1988. *Songs of the Saints of
India*. New York: Oxford University Press.

denying the sanctity of their scriptures and the efficacy of their rituals. He especially condemned as idiotic and cruel the sacrifice of animals.

Dadu eventually moved to Amber, on the road from Jaipur, where he lived in a cave below the Amber Palace. Stories recount how Raja Bhagavan Das, who lived in the palace, introduced him to Emperor Akbar. One of the pictorial representations in most Dadu Panth temples shows Dadu seated on a cloud, Akbar at his feet. Later Dadu moved to Kalyanapura, then after another period of wandering, settled at Naraina, where he died in 1604. His students took his body to a hill at nearby Bhairana, and left it exposed to the elements.

Dadu's poetry is indebted to Kabir and others of the Sant tradition. Like Kabir he composed both padas and sakhis. He did not write down his songs or sayings, which were recorded by disciples. Monika Thiel-Horstmann, who has produced a reader of Braj Bhasa—the Rajasthani dialect of Dadu's verse—finds his poetry unremarkable. It adds little to a tradition, she says, that was already over 200 years old. In this sense he would not be, in Ezra Pound's terms, a 'founder', but rather a consolidator of poetic discoveries that preceded him.

## Sakhis

I tell the truth,
there's no doubt about it—
whoever takes the life of another creature
goes the dark
road to hell. (13.4)

They cut animal throats, says Dadu—
and claim it's their faith.
Five times a day at their prayers
standing on nothing. (13.10)

The Lord of Wisdom, says Dadu
throws dice.
Nobody watches him.
He rules the universe and
you can't stain him. (35.5)

There's a worm called Time
drilling into your body.
Every day, says Dadu, the end
draws closer.                                                      (25.12)

He wouldn't hurt his relatives
but heretics he'd kill.
Dadu says: you won't see the light
if you don't
kill yourself.                                                      (13.4)

The worn-out clay pitcher is broken
that once had nine holes.
Did you imagine, asks Dadu,
it held water forever?                                              (25.7)

                    *—Revised from the translation by Monika Thiel-Horstmann**

# Punjabi Songs

In 1913, the Old Bourne Press released a limited edition volume of 405 copies entitled *Thirty Indian Songs*. Its type hand-set, its cover in austere blue boards, the book deliberately carried the look of the Arts and Crafts Movement spearheaded in England by William Morris, and may have been printed on one of Morris's former Kelmscot Press hand-presses. Messrs Luzac and Sons of Great Russell Street, the preeminent bookstore for Asian material in London, sold *Thirty Indian Songs*. It contained Punjabi and Kashmiri lyrics the art historian Ananda Coomaraswamy and his English wife, Ratan Devi, had recorded from singers during a stay in Kashmir. Coomaraswamy—his father Sri Lankan, his mother English—spent his life collecting and writing about Indian art, eventually moving to the United States where he assembled the first collection of India's art in North America, at the Boston Museum of Fine Arts.

---

* Thiel-Horstmann, Monika. 1983. *Crossing the Ocean of Existence: Braj Bhasa Religious Poetry from Rajasthan*. Wiesbaden: Otto Harrasowitz.

*Thirty Indian Songs* had a foreword by Rabindranath Tagore. In fact, Coomaraswamy had been friendly with various members of the Bengali Renaissance; paintings he received from its members are also housed in the Boston Museum collection. His translations—which like so much bhakti verse lie on the cusp between devotion and love song—are examples of the type of neo-Victorian translation about to vanish from England and America. Modernism would sweep off the grammatical inversions ('there meets me the young boy'), capitalized *Thee* and *Thou*, and other archaisms. But Coomaraswamy's translations are classics of their sort.

Coomaraswamy gives an account of the singer, Ustad Abdul Rahim, from whom he received the songs in their original Punjabi:

His ancestors were Brahmans, forcibly converted at the time of Aurangzeb. Like many other Panjabi Musulmans in the same case, the family retain many Hindu customs, e.g., non-remarriage of widows. Abdul Rahim's faith in Hindu gods is as strong as his belief in Islam and Moslem saints, and he sings with equal earnestness of Krishna or Allah, exemplifying the complete fusion of Hindu and Moslem tradition characteristic of so many parts of northern India today. He is devout and even superstitious; he would hesitate to sing *dipak rag*, unless in very cold weather.

I

When I go down to draw water, O Mother, at Jamna ghat
He catches my clothes and twists my hand—
When I go to sell milk,
At every step Gokula seeks to stop me.
He is so obstinate, what can I say?
He ever comes and goes: why does this Youngling so?
He seizes my arm and shuts my mouth and holds me close:
I will make my complaint to Kans Raja, then I shall have no fear of Thee!

II

See, Sakhis, how Krishna stands!
How can I go fetch water, my mother-in-law?
When I go to draw water from Jamna,
There meets me the young boy of Nand!

### III

What yogi is this, with rings in his ears and ashes smeared, who
  wanders about?
Some perform meditation, some dwell in the woods, some call on
  Thy name with devotion!

### IV

*To the hem of thy garment I cling, O Rama!*
My refuge Thou art:
Thou art my Lord—
*To the hem of thy garment I cling, O Rama!*

### V

How can I loosen the knot that binds the heart of my beloved?
All my comrades well-decked are embraced by their lovers,
But I sit alone eating poison.

### VI

My Lord has not spoken, he sulks since the afternoon—
*The wheat crops are ripe, the rose trees in bloom.*
I need not thy earnings, only come to the Panjab again!
Thou farest away on thy journey, but I am left desolate:
Oh! the empty house and the courtyard fill me with fear—
*The wheat crops are ripe, the rose trees in bloom.*

—*Translated by Ananda K. Coomaraswamy*[*]

* Coomaraswamy, Ananda K. 1913. *Thirty Indian Songs.* London: Olde Bourne Press.

# EAST

# Vaishnava Poetry

## Jayadeva

The twelfth-century *Gita-govinda* of Jayadeva is widely regarded as the last great poem in the Sanskrit language. It holds two other distinctions. One is that it appears to be the first full-blown account in literature of Radha as Krishna's favourite among the gopis or cowgirls of Vrindavan. Secondly, it seems to be the first historical instance of poetry being written with specified ragas to which its lyrics are to be sung. The poem presents the love affair of Krishna and Radha as a cycle, from initial 'secret desires' and urgent lovemaking, to separation—nights of betrayal, mistrust, longing, feverish urges—and, finally, to a consummation that is spiritual as well as carnal. At this remove from Jayadeva's century, who can tell if he meant his poetry cycle as an allegory of the human spirit's dark night and final illumination? That is how it gets read though.

Jayadeva's *Gita-govinda* has been called an 'opera'. It is comprised of twelve cantos or chapters, with twenty-four songs distributed through them. Narrative verse, composed in Sanskrit kavya form and metre, connects the songs. The twenty-four songs, with their repeating refrains, resemble nothing from the earlier Sanskrit tradition. Jayadeva took their rhythms from folk sources; the songs occur in end-rhymed couplets (almost unknown to Sanskrit court tradition), each couplet then followed by a repeating line, a refrain that sums up the emotion or action of the entire song. In this way the *Gita-govinda* straddles high-art Sanskrit poetry and the local, vernacular traditions that would follow. For centuries the *Gita-govinda* has been performed, especially in Orissa, with dancers, costume, music, and stage settings. It is also considered a sacred text, and in the fifteenth century was instituted as the sole liturgy for the Sri Jagannatha temple in Puri.

Jayadeva's birthplace is uncertain—some think Orissa, some Mithila, some Bengal. Accounts of his life say he was a carefully trained poet, in the Sanskrit mode, when he took a vow to wander as a homeless mendicant, and sleep no more than a single night under any tree. On this endless pilgrimage he passed through Puri, where the chief administrator of the Jagannatha temple had a vision that Jayadeva should marry his daughter, a dancer dedicated to the temple, settle down, and compose a devotional poem to Krishna. The daughter's name may have been Padmavati—a name that appears in one of the *Gita-govinda*'s opening verses. Jayadeva complied. He renounced his vows, married the girl, and wrote his poem.

Meeting Padmavati wakened in Jayadeva the *rasa* of love. His poem never divides the rasa into erotic or spiritual modes. What might have seemed distant accounts of spiritual grace, a theme for poetry and folksong, or even an abstract religious doctrine, came alive in his own body: the merging of spiritual and erotic ecstasy. Later poets would sing of the *prem-bhakti-marg*, the path of love and devotion, and warn of its razor sharp edge. But under Padmavati's hands Jayadeva learnt that the old tales, the yogic teachings, were no abstract affair. They are an experience tasted through one's own senses, its rhythms and phases available to anyone.

In his poem Krishna appears desperately human. An underlying cadence suggests he is the driving force of wild nature—Eros incarnate— but his acutely human emotions give the poem poignance. In another sphere, the cosmic realm of Vaishnava devotion, Krishna remains the final resort for humans in the Kali Yuga, a time when older techniques of yoga, meditation, or worship may be out of human reach. One's own body, wracked as it is by desire and loneliness, is the sole vehicle for salvation and Krishna the only refuge. Radha, meanwhile, may be something like a spirit of nature, dancing with anguish and ecstasy in our glands. For her, 'erotic' or 'spiritual' would be meaningless distinctions as she sets out, spurred by relentless desire, to the dark grove of *tamala* trees where her lover waits. She is pure life-force, the spirit within us, that yearns to give love in a dark, cruel era.

The following verses, mostly drawn from the more 'classical' narrative stanzas, reproduce the cycle of the poem as Jayadeva conceived it.

## *From the* Gita-govinda

'Clouds thicken the sky,
the forests are
dark with tamala trees.
He is afraid of night, Radha,
take him home.'
They depart at Nanda's directive
passing on the way
thickets of trees.
But reaching Yamuna River, secret desires
overtake Radha and Krishna.                                              (i.2)

Jayadeva, chief poet on pilgrimage
to Padmavati's feet—
every craft of
Goddess Language
stored in his heart—
has assembled tales from the erotic encounters
of Krishna and Shri
to compose these cantos.                                                 (i.4)

If thoughts of Krishna
    make your heart moody;
if arts of courtship
    stir something deep;
Then listen to Jayadeva's songs
    flooded with tender music.                                           (i.46)

Krishna stirs every
creature on earth.

Archaic longing awakens.
He initiates Love's
holy rite with languorous blue
lotus limbs.
Cowherd girls like
splendid wild animals draw him into their
bodies for pleasure—
It is spring. Krishna at play
is eros incarnate.                                    (ii.1)

Krishna roamed the forest
taking the cowherdesses one after
another for love.
Radha's hold slackened,
jealousy drove her far off.
But over each refuge
in the vine-draped thickets
swarmed a loud circle of bees.
Miserable
she confided the secret
to her friend—                                       (ii.10)

## Radha speaks

My conflicted heart
treasures even his infidelities.
Won't admit anger.
Forgives the deceptions.
Secret desires rise in my breasts.
What can I do? Krishna
hungry for lovers
slips off without me.
This torn heart grows only
more ardent.                                          (ii.19)

His hand loosens from the
bamboo flute.

A tangle of pretty
eyes draws him down.
Moist excitement on his cheeks.
Krishna catches me
eyeing him in a grove
swarmed by young women—
I stare at his smiling baffled face
and get aroused.

(iii.14)

## Krishna speaks

Every touch brought a new thrill.
Her eyes darted wildly.
From her mouth the
fragrance of lotus,
a rush of sweet forbidden words.
A droplet of juice
on her crimson lower lip.
My mind fixes these absent
sensations in a *samadhi*—
How is it that parted from her
the oldest
wound breaks open?

(iv.10)

## Radha's messenger speaks

Her house has become
a pulsating jungle.
Her circle of girlfriends
a tightening snare.
Each time she breathes
a sheet of flame
bursts above the trees.
Krishna, you have gone—
in your absence she takes shape

as a doe crying out—
while Love turns to Death
& closes in
on tiger paws.                                                    (iv.20)

Sick with feverish
urges.
Only the poultice of your body
can heal her, holy physician of the heart.
Free her from torment, Krishna—
or are you
cruel as a thunderbolt?                                           (v.7)


## The messenger speaks to Radha

Krishna lingers
in the thicket
where together you mastered the secrets
of lovemaking.
Fixed in meditation,
sleepless
he chants a sequence of mantras.
He has one burning desire—
to draw *amrita*
from your offered breasts.                                        (v.16)

Sighs, short repeated gasps—
he glances around helpless.
The thicket deserted.
He pushes back in, his breath
comes in a rasp.
He rebuilds the couch of blue floral branches.
Steps back and studies it.
Radha, precious Radha!
Your lover turns on a wheel,
image after
feverish image.                                                   (vi.11)

She ornaments her limbs
if a single leaf stirs
in the forest.
She thinks it's you, folds back
the bedclothes and stares
in rapture for hours.
Her heart conceives a hundred
amorous games on the well-prepared bed.
But without you this
wisp of a girl
will fade
to nothing tonight.                                    (vii.1)

At nightfall
the crater-pocked moon as though
exposing a crime
slips onto the paths of
girls who seek lovers.
It casts a platinum web
over Vrindavan forest's dark hollows—
a sandalwood spot
on the proud face of sky.                              (vii.2)

The brindled moon soars above.
Krishna waits underneath.
And Radha
wrenched with grief
is alone.                                              (vii.21)

The lonely moon
pale as Krishna's sad, far-off
lotus-face has
calmed my thoughts.
O but the moon is also Love's planet—
a wild desolation
strikes through my heart.                              (x.10)

Let the old doubts go,
anguished Radha.

Your unfathomed breasts and
cavernous loins
are all I desire.
What other girl has the power?
Love is a ghost
that has slipped into my entrails.
When I reach to embrace your
deep breasts
may we fulfill the rite
we were born for—                                          (xi.1)

Krishna for hours
entreated
the doe-eyed girl
then returned to his thicket bed & dressed.
Night fell again.
Radha, unseen, put on radiant gems.
A girlish voice pressed her—
*go swiftly.*                                               (xi. 10)


## Her companion reports—

'She'll look into me—
tell love tales—
chafing with pleasure she'll draw me—
into her body—
*drakshyati vakshyati ramsyate'*
    —he's fearful,
    he glances about. He shivers for you,
bristles, calls wildly, sweats, goes forward,
reels back.
The dark thicket closes
about him.                                                 (xi.11)

Eyes dark with kohl
ears bright with creamy tamala petals
a black lotus headdress & breasts

traced with musk-leaf—
In every thicket, friend,
Night's precious cloak wraps a girl's limbs.
The veiled affairs
    the racing heart ...                (xi.23)

Eager, fearful, ecstatic—
darting her eyes across Govinda she
enters the thicket.
Ankles ringing with silver.

Her friends have slipped off.
Her lower lip's moist
wistful, chaste, swollen, trembling, deep.
He sees her raw heart
sees her eyes rest on the couch of
fresh flowering twigs
& speaks.                  (xii.1)

## Sung to Raga Vibhasa

*Come, Radha, come. Krishna follows your*
*every desire.*

'Soil my bed with indigo footprints, *Kamini,*
lay waste the grove
savage it with your petal-soft feet.

'I take your feet in lotus hands, *Kamini,*
you have come far.
Lay these gold flaring anklets across my bed.

'Let *yes yes* flow from your mouth like *amrita.*
From your breasts, *Kamini,*
I draw off the *dukula*-cloth. We are no longer separate.'  (xii.2, 3, 4)

## Sung to Raga Ramakari

*She sings while Krishna plays, her heart drawn*
*into ecstasy—*

'On my breast, your hand Krishna
cool as sandalwood. Draw a leaf wet with deer musk here,
it is Love's sacramental jar.

Drape my loins with jeweled belts, fabric & gemstones.
My *mons venus* is brimming with nectar,
a cave mouth for thrusts of Desire.'                    (xii.18)

Reader, open your heart
to Jayadeva's well-
crafted poem.
Krishna's deeds lie in your memory now—
*amrita* to salve
    a Dark Age's pestilence.                    (xii.19)

*On my breast draw a leaf*
*paint my cheeks*
*lay a silk scarf across these dark loins.*
*Wind into my heavy black braid*
*white petals,*
*fit gemstones onto my wrists,*
*anklets over my feet.*
And each thing she desired
her saffron robed lover
fulfilled.                    (xii.20)

—*Translated by Andrew Schelling**

* Schelling, Andrew. 2007. *Kamini: A Cycle of Poems from Jayadeva's Gita-govinda.*
St. Louis: emdash studios.

# Songs from the Bengali

With the *Gita-govinda*, Jayadeva set the tone in eastern India for songs of the love affair of Radha and Krishna. Jayadeva's poem, sometimes called an opera, has in recent centuries been performed with ritual dance, musical orchestra, elaborate costumes, and stage settings. It is a dramatic work, with an adherence to the full cycle of the love between Krishna and Radha. The inheritors of Jayadeva's vision, far from the world of Sanskrit court poetry, sang differently. Though every aspect of their songs echoes or recuperates a mood Jayadeva explored, the vernacular bhakti poets did not sing *of* a drama so much as they sang from *within* it. Vidyapati, Chandidasa, and numerous others made two significant changes. First, each of their songs stands complete in itself, and never depends on being situated in a cycle of songs or dramatic performance. Secondly, these poets produced *lyric* poems, not narrative—sung in the first person—which has the impact of coming directly from the poet's personal emotions. The singer may take the part of Radha, or of one of the messengers that slips between the lovers, but the poet assumes the role or puts on the mask to get at his own emotions. You do not need a larger narrative to feel the passion.

The translators—Edward C. Dimock, Jr., a Bengali scholar, and American poet Denise Levertov—selected thirty-four separate poems from the Bengali, taken from a variety of poets. They presented these as a cycle, similar to Jayadeva's. Notice the presence of Vidyapati here—who most likely composed his songs in Maithili. There are old Bengali versions of his songs, and he fits well with Chandidasa, Jnana-dasa, and others. In presenting seventeen of the Dimock–Levertov translations, I have tried to maintain the feel of a cycle, or cyclic performance, which was their intention. Notice the final song's shift of perspective: into a vision of death and dissolution. The poet leaves behind the drama of Krishna and Radha, and his lyric becomes both excruciatingly personal and profoundly cosmic.

The girl and the woman
bound in one being:

the girl puts up her hair,
the woman lets it
fall to cover her breasts;
the girl reveals her arms,
her long legs, innocently bold;
the woman wraps her shawl modestly about her,
her open glance a little veiled.
Restless feet, a blush on the young breasts,
hint at her heart's disquiet:
behind her closed eyes
Kama awakes, born in imagination, the god.

*Vidyapati says, O Krishna, bridegroom,*
*be patient, she will be brought to you.*                              (7)


Fingering the border of her friend's sari, nervous and
            afraid,
sitting tensely on the edge of Krishna's couch,

as her friend left she too looked to go
but in desire Krishna blocked her way.

He was infatuated, she bewildered;
he was clever, and she naïve.

He put out his hand to touch her; she quickly pushed
            it away.
He looked into her face, her eyes filled with tears.

He held her forcefully, she trembled violently
and hid her face from his kisses behind the edge of
            her sari.

Then she lay down, frightened, beautiful as a doll;
he hovered like a bee round a lotus in a painting.

*Govinda-dasa says, Because of this,*
*drowned in the well of her beauty,*
*Krishna's lust was changed.*                                        (11)

Love, I take on splendor in your splendor,
grace and gentleness are mine because of your
        beauty.

I remember
how I embraced your feet, holding them
tight to my breast.

Others have many loves, I have
only you,
dearer to me than life.
You are the kohl on my eyes, the ornaments
on my body,
you, dark moon.

*Jnana-dasa says, Your love*
*binds heart to heart.*                                    (16)


My friend, I cannot answer when you ask me to
        explain
what has befallen me.
Love is transformed, renewed,
each moment.
He has dwelt in my eyes all the days of my life,
yet I am not sated with seeing.
My ears have heard his sweet voice in eternity,
and yet it is always new to them.
How many honeyed nights have I passed with him
in love's bliss, yet my body
wonders at his.
Through all the ages
he has been clasped to my breast,
yet my desire
never abates.
I have seen subtle people sunk in passion
but none came so close to the heart of the fire.

*Who shall be found to cool your heart,*
*says Vidyapati.*                                          (18)

When they had made love
she lay in his arms in the *kunja* grove.
Suddenly she called his name
and wept—as if she burned in the fire of
separation.
>The gold was in her *anchal*
>but she looked afar for it!
—Where has he gone? Where has my love gone?
O why has he left me alone?
And she writhed on the ground in despair,
only her pain kept her from fainting.
Krishna was astonished
and could not speak.

*Taking her beloved friend by the hand,*
*Govinda-dasa led her softly away.*                    (23)


## To her friend

O, why did I go to the Yamuna river? There
the moon apple of Nanda's eye lay waiting
under the *kadamba* tree.
The honey of his look, the radiance
of his body—these
were the bait and the snare he laid:
and my eyes lit there like birds
and at once were trapped,
and my heart leapt like a doe into his nets
leaving the cage of my breast empty,
and goaded by his glance,
my pride, that wild elephant,
which I had kept
chained night and day in my mind, broke loose
and escaped me.
>At the first note of his flute
down came the lion gate of reverence for elders,

down came the door of *dharma*,
my guarded treasure of modesty was lost,
I was thrust to the ground as if by a thunderbolt.
Ah, yes, his dark body
poised in the *tribhanga* pose
shot the arrow that pierced me;
no more honor, my family
lost to me,
my home at Vraja
lost to me.
Only my life is left—and my life too
is only a breath that is leaving me.

*So says Jagadananda-dasa.*                                    (28)


## To her friend

My mind is not on housework.
Now I weep, now I laugh at the world's
censure.
        He draws me—to become
an outcast, a hermit woman in the woods!
He has bereft me of parents, brothers, sisters,
my good name. His flute
took my heart—
his flute, a thin bamboo trap enclosing me—
a cheap bamboo flute was Radha's ruin.
That hollow, simple stick—
fed nectar by his lips, but issuing
poisons ...

If you should find
a clump of jointed reeds,
pull off their branches!
Tear them up by the roots!
Throw them
        into the sea.

*Dvija Chandidasa says, Why the bamboo?*
*Not it but Krishna enthralls you: him you cannot*
        *uproot.*                                          (30)


## To Krishna

*A wicked woman—fouler than the foulest poison.*
So his mother's cruelty, like fire
burning in me.
My tyrant husband: the whetted
edge of a razor. And all around me,
reproachful dutiful women.
My love, what shall I tell you?
Whatever their calumnies, you
are my life itself.
        My body
bears your brand—they know it.
For shame I cannot raise my head
        before chaste women,
I cannot bear the cruelty, the knife-thrust
of seeing my fellow women make mocking signs to
        me.
I have weighed it all.
        Yet I have chosen
to endure abuse for your sake.

*So Balarama-dasa says.*                                  (33)


## The messenger replies

When you listened to the sound
of Krishna's flute,
I stopped your ears.
When you gazed at the beauty
of his body,
I covered your eyes.

You were angry.
O lovely one, I told you then
that if you let love grow in you
your life would pass in tears.
You offered him your body,
you wanted his touch—
you did not ask if he would be kind.
And now each day your beauty
fades a little more;
how much longer can you live?
You planted in your heart
the tree of love,
in hope of nourishment
from that dark cloud.
Now water it
with your tears,

*says Govinda-dasa.*                                      (42)


I who body and soul
am at your beck and call,
was a girl of noble family.
I took no thought of what would be said of me,
I abandoned everything:
now I am part of you,
your will is my will.
O Madhava, never let our love
seem to grow stale—
I beg you, let the dew
not dry on our flowers,
that my honor not be destroyed.

When he heard these words from her beautiful
        mouth, Madhava
bowed his head. He knew he held
the flower of her life in his keeping.

*Vidyapati*                                              (51)

## Her friend speaks

Her cloud of hair eclipses the luster of her face,
    like Rahu greedy for the moon;
the garland glitters in her unbound hair, a wave of
    the Ganges in the waters of the Yamuna.
How beautiful the deliberate, sensuous union of the
    two; the girl playing this time the active
    role,
riding her lover's outstretched body in delight;
her smiling lips shine with drops of sweat; the god
    of love offering pearls to the moon.
She of beautiful face hotly kisses the mouth of her
    beloved; the moon, with face bent down,
    drinks of the lotus.
The garlands hanging on her heavy breast seem like
    a stream of milk from golden jars.
The tinkling bells which decorate her hips sound the
    triumphal music of the god of love.

*Vidyapati*                                              (56)

## She speaks

Beloved, what more shall I say to you?
In life and in death, in birth after birth
you are the lord of my life.
A noose of love binds
my heart to your feet.
My mind fixed on you alone, I have offered you
            everything;
in truth, I have become your slave.
In this family, in that house, who is really mine?
Whom can I call my own?
It was bitter cold, and I took refuge
at your lotus feet.

While my eyes blink, and I do not see you,
I feel the heart within me die.

*A touchstone*
*I have threaded and wear upon my throat,*
*says Chandidasa.*                                          (57)


O my friend, my sorrow is unending.
It is the rainy season, my house is empty,
the sky is filled with seething clouds,
the earth sodden with rain,
and my love far away.

Cruel Kama pierces me with his arrows:
the lightning flashes, the peacocks dance,
frogs and waterbirds, drunk with delight,
call incessantly—and my heart is heavy.
Darkness on earth,
the sky intermittently lit with a sullen glare ...

*Vidyapati says,*
*How will you pass this night without your lord?*           (61)


When my beloved returns to my house
I shall make my body a temple of gladness,
I shall make my body the altar of joy
and let down my hair to sweep it.
My twisting necklace of pearls shall be the intricate
sprinkled design on the altar,
my full breasts the water jars,
my curved hips the plaintain trees,
the tinkling bells at my waist the young shoots of the
        mango.
I shall use the arcane arts of fair women in all lands
to make my beauty outshine a thousand moons.

*Soon your hopes, O Radha, says Vidyapati,*
*will be fulfilled, and he will be at your side.*            (65)

*Children, wife, friend—*
*drops of water on heated sand.*
*I spent myself on them, forgetting you.*
*What are they to me now,*
*O Madhava, now that I am old and without hope,*
*apart from you. But you are the savior of the world*
*and full of mercy.*
        *Half my life I passed in sleep—*
*my youth, now my old age,*
*how much time.*
*I spent my youth in lust and dissipation.*
*I had no time to worship you.*
        *Ageless gods*
*have come and passed away.*
*Born from you, they enter you again*
*like waves into the sea.*
*For you have no beginning, and no end.*
            *Now*
*at the end, I fear*
*the messengers of Death.*
*Apart from you, there is no way.*
*I call you Lord,*
*the infinite and finite,*
*my salvation.*

Vidyapati                                                      (69)

*—Translated by  Edward C. Dimock, Jr. and Denise Levertov**

* Dimock, Edward C., Jr. and Denise Levertov. 1967. *In Praise of Krishna: Songs from the Bengali.* Garden City, New York: Anchor Books.

# Vidyapati

Vidyapati was born in 1352 at Bisapi, a village in the district of eastern Bihar known as Madhubani. His father was a courtier of Hindu kings who made their court near present-day Darbhanga, and likely through his father's connections Vidyapati entered the service of Kirti Simha, the Maithil king who reigned in the period 1380–1390. A good Sanskrit scholar, Vidyapati wrote a long poem in Sanskrit, partly to glorify his king—the *Kirtilata* or 'Vine of Glory', Kirti (Fame, Glory) being his patron's name. In the opening verse he states that poetry is composed in every house; listeners dwell in every village; critics thrive in every town; but patrons exist almost nowhere.

When Kirti Simha's son, Deva Simha, assumed rulership, Vidyapati began residence at the court. During that time he pioneered a new literature—switching from the brahmin's Sanskrit to Maithili, the vernacular, a shift much like Dante's decision at nearly the same time to compose in Italian instead of Latin. Vidyapati wrote more than 500 love songs, spurred by a keen friendship with Deva Simha. Behind those poems in Maithili, as W.G. Archer has stated, 'lay a whole tradition of Indian love-making.' Vidyapati was well versed in Sanskrit secular poetry, particularly its immersion of human sexual love in details of the natural world. Throughout his songs, the lovers are never alone, but the moon, the rivers, the birds, bees, lotuses, trees, vines, and rushes are animated by the same passion and rapture as humans. 'The sky fell with my dress', and 'the moon seized her', feel ordinary in Vidyapati's poems. Through such images echo the shamanic voices of thousands of years of Euro-Asiatic singing—the power of song that links humans to the irrevocable cycles of nature.

In the twelfth century, two hundred years before Vidyapati, an enormous change had overtaken eastern India. The love affair of Krishna and Radha emerged as a powerful religious revival. The lovemaking of the dark god and his favourite *gopi*, Radha, came to be seen as—not just a symbol—but the equivalent of the self's union with god, the cosmic drama that plays out in each individual's heart. To love Krishna was to achieve salvation, and in the Kali Yuga, many claimed, this was the only salvation left. Praise of love became worship of Krishna, and erotic desire became the vehicle of worship. In Orissa, Jayadeva had composed the last great Sanskrit poem, the *Gita-govinda*, and its influence on Vidyapati was enormous. Vidyapati saw sexual love as the deepest need and profoundest experience a human can undergo. Simply to experience desire, sexual pleasure, or romantic anguish, draws one into the sphere of Krishna. In his poems even jealousy, grief, or frustration, become pure emotions—rasas—providing an approach to Krishna.

Vidyapati composed his Krishna–Radha poems in the Maithili language from about 1380 until 1406, the year his patron Siva Simha vanished after a military defeat at Muslim hands. Though he lived until 1448, Vidyapati wrote mostly complicated treatises in Sanskrit during his last forty years. This leaves many wondering how sincere his devotion to Krishna was. Are his songs really just erotic verse, dressed out in the stories of Krishna and Radha? Or are they devotional songs, modelled on the Sanskrit court poetry in which he had trained? At this point, only the spirit of the poems can tell us. The translations here are by Deben Bhattacharya, the Bengali musicologist, filmmaker, poet, and field recorder. He once wrote:

The greatness of Vidyapati's songs depends on the fusion of natural phenomena such as lightning and clouds, the moon and the night lily, the lotus and the bee with the greatest of lovers, Radha and Krishna and their emotional reactions to love, anguish, passion, jealousy, joy and sorrow.

It is worth noting that Vidyapati's patron assigned to the poet a singer—named Jayata—who determined the raga each song should be set to. Dancing girls at the court learnt the lyrics, and his songs spread across Mithila.

> There was a shudder in her whispering voice.
> She was shy to frame her words.
> What has happened tonight to lovely Radha?
> Now she consents, now she is afraid.
> When asked for love, she closes her eyes,
> Eager to reach the ocean of desire.
> He begs her for a kiss.
> She turns her mouth away

And then, like a night lily, the moon seized her.
She felt his touch startling her girdle.
She knew her love treasure was being robbed.
With her dress she covered up her breasts.
The treasure was left uncovered.

Vidyapati wonders at the neglected bed.
Lovers are busy in each other's arms.

O friend, I cannot tell you
Whether he was near or far, real or a dream.
Like a vine of lightning,
As I chained the dark one,
I felt a river flooding in my heart.
Like a shining moon,
I devoured that liquid face.
I felt stars shooting around me.
The sky fell with my dress,
Leaving my ravished breasts.
I was rocking like the earth.
In my storming breath
I could hear my ankle bells,
Sounding like bees.
Drowned in the last waters of dissolution,
I knew that this was not the end.

Says Vidyapati:
How can I possibly believe such nonsense?

O friend, how can I say what happened in the night?
Madhava was torture.
Thrusting his fingers on my breasts
He drank my lips.
Pressing his face hard on mine,
He took my life away.
His youthful strength
So wantonly aroused

Drugged his senses.
A country boy,
He did not know
The art of love.
I prayed and begged in vain.

Vidyapati says:
My dear lady,
You are enchanted by that greedy god.


He left me saying he would be back tomorrow.
I've covered the floor of my home
Writing: Tomorrow.
When dawn came, they all enquired:
Tell us, friend,
When will your tomorrow come?
Tomorrow, tomorrow, I gave up my hopes,
My beloved never returned.

Says Vidyapati, listen, beautiful one,
Other women held him back.


O friend:
How can you ask me
What I feel?
In talk, love always grows,
Is always new.
Since I was born
I've seen his beauty
With insatiate eyes.
His gentle voice
Brushed my ears.
Thrilled, I long for more.
Nights of spring
Passed in joy,
Yet still the game of love
Has new delights.

I've held him to my heart
A million ages,
Yet longing flares again.
A host of lovers,
Their love reduced to ashes,
Know nothing of its power ...


How the rain falls
In deadly darkness!
O gentle girl, the rain
Pours on your path
And roaming spirits straddle the wet night.
She is afraid
Of loving for the first time.
O Madhava,
Cover her with sweetness.

How will she cross the fearful river
In her path?
Enraptured with love,
Beloved Radha is careless of the rest.

Knowing so much,
O shameless one,
How can you be cold towards her?
Whoever saw
Honey fly to the bee?


Tell me what to do.
Even the bed of water-drenched lotuses
Dries up as he reclines.
The coolness of sandal paste
Is no remedy,
Nor the hostile moon.

Be sure, O beautiful one,
Krishna pines away
From wanting you.

Day by day his body grows thin.
His heart ignores all others.
The doctors have left him
Without hope,
His only medicine
The nectar of your lips.

If I go I lose my home,
If I stay I lose my love ...
The enemy moon
Wickedly bars my way.
The sky is bright from end to end.
Thinking it was dark,
I set out on my way
And then it rose
In its provoking form.
Who can control the demon moon?
But I must keep my tryst
With Krishna.

Her hair, disheveled,
Veils the beauty of her face
As evil shadows eat the glowing moon.
Strings of blossom in her hair
Wantonly play
As flooded rivers
Twine about their twins.

Exquisite today,
This sport of love,
As Radha rides on Krishna.
Beads of sweat glisten on her face
Like pearls on the moon,
A present to her
From the god of love.

With all her force
She kisses her lover's lips,

Like the moon swooping
To drink a lotus bloom.
Her necklace dangles
Below her hanging breasts,
Like streams of milk
Trickling from golden jars.
The jingling bells around her waist
Sang glory to the god of love.


There is the one and only moon,
And then the moon
That haloes the crown of Siva.
There are people with the name 'Moon'.

I saw one moon in the sky
But there were three with you.
That exquisite sight of the night
Confused my heart.

Who could believe
That there are moons and moons,
Held in a single place?

Which is the moon of stars
And which the moon among girls,
And which moon shines
On the feathers of the night birds?

One moon plays with Madhava
And another in the sky.


Has then my lover been suborned by others?
Has he succumbed to yet another girl
Who also knows the ways of love?
What evil course has turned the gods against me
That Krishna never even says my name?
O friend, tell me what to do.
He lives in the same village

Yet might be in another land.
The god of love lassoes me with hope.
Only with death do girls abandon longing.
O when will end these days of waiting?
Youth is unstable, life so short.


Seeing the bright moon
Betray the path,
She bent her face
And cried aloud.
She took mascara from her eyes
And painted Rahu
Eating the moon.
O Madhava,
In a foreign land
Harsh is the heart.
Come back.
I have seen your loved one
Frightened of the god of love.
She calls on Siva
Again and again,
Writhing in the dust,
Offering
Her breasts and hands.
Her body once clutched by your fingers,
She cannot bear the southern breeze.
Gone is her life yet hope teases her
And still she plays
With the fangs of a snake.


New to love,
I shrank from loving,
Yet the night grew
And all was done.
I did not relish
Sweets of dalliance.

My shyness warred against my will …
He seized my garland,
Held my hair
And pressed his heart
Against my smothered breasts
But, in my clumsy innocence,
Alone, with none to aid,
I could not please.
He wanted everything
In one great rapture
And to my painful shame
I gave so little.
The spell of passion went.
I said
Nothing.


Do not abandon
her delicate limbs
For fear of crushing.
Who has ever seen
A blossom smothered
By the weight of a bee?
Madhava, mark my words:
Do not hold back
If she cries 'No, no',
Or futile comes the dawn.
With your ardent kissing
Give her lips
The hue of dusk
And slowly bring her
To the height of joy.
The play of love,
Its keen delights,
Should grow and grow
Like the white brilliance
Of a waxing moon.

Krishna, if you touch me by force,
The guilt of murder will be on your hands.
O master.of love,
you are stubborn with experience.
I do not know whether
Love is bitter or sweet.
It makes me shudder
When I hear of love ...

Says Vidyapati:
If I know the truth,
A fruit is not sweet when green.


So long our world was new,
We were one like fish and water.
Such was our love.
A sharp word passed between us.
My dear love smiled
And gave no answer.
Krishna, in the same bed with me,
Seemed in a far-away land.
In the forest where no one moves,
My love now smiles,
My love now speaks.
I shall dress as a *yogini*
And look for my love.


Hold my hand.
Caress me, Krishna.'
I will give you
A wondrous garland.
The friends are gone,
But which way, Krishna,
I do not know.
I will not walk
with you, Krishna,

But at the river
By the lonely bank
There I will meet you.

*—Translated by Deben Bhattacharya**

# Chandidas

For over five centuries songs have circulated in Bengal with the name
Chandidas attached. When scholars winnow through, and locate poems
that may be traced authentically to a historical figure of the fifteenth
century, they still find poems composed by four figures of that name:
Chandidas, Dwija Chandidas, Badu Chandidas, and Dina Chandidas.
Whether these were four separate poets or only one is uncertain. The
Chandidas story that circulates with the songs portrays him as the chief
*rasika* bhakta, or devotee of love—pure, untarnished love. Unlike many
other bhakti poets—such as Vidyapati—Chandidas seems little touched
by the influence of Sanskrit poetry. Almost all of his poetry speaks in
the voice of Radha or Krishna, burning in a fever of desire. But it is
remarkably free of standard literary figures, and the depth of longing
blazes through every poem.

Chandidas seems to have been from Nanur, a village in the Birbhum
region of Bengal. His translator, Deben Bhattacharya, states that
Jayadeva hailed from the same district. Bhattacharya goes on to say,
'The history of Jayadeva repeated itself in Rabindranath Tagore, the
most celebrated poet of this [the twentieth] century ... Between these
two literary giants of very different centuries from Birbhum, Chandidas
enjoys the distinction of being the father of Bengali poetry.' The story of
Jayadeva seems in some respects repeated in Chandidas as well.

A brahmin, dedicated to the temple of the local goddess, Bashuli,
Chandidas fell in love with a young woman named Rami who had
appeared at the temple. Rami, however, was a low-caste washerwoman,

---

* Bhattacharya, Deben. 1970. *Love Songs of Vidyapati*. Edited by W.G. Archer.
New York: Grove Press.

scrubbing the courtyard, and the affair scandalized the village. To complicate Chandidas's story—and who he was or who wrote the lyrics—many of his poems are in Radha's voice. Which means they articulate the viewpoint of, or were even written by, Rami.

> I throw ashes at all laws
> Made by man or god.
> What is the worth
> Of your vile laws
> That failed me
> In love?

Chandidas perfected the bhakti path known as *madhurya*, 'honeyed'. This is the method of worship which uses the poet's own bodily experience, and the explosive power of the emotions, as the channel for union with god. From the earliest period of Sanskrit poetry (200–400 CE), the most potent emotion was known to be *sringara*, erotic love. Chandidas—and following him, the Bauls—insist on living out the kinds of events and emotions that to most people remain only stories.

In his essay 'Sahaja', touching on Chandidas, Ananda Coomaraswamy writes: 'In India we could not escape the conviction that sexual love has a deep and spiritual significance. There is nothing with which we can better compare the "mystic vision" of the finite with its infinite ambient.' Considering the violations of caste, ritual, and common sense, that permeate Chandidas's life, Coomaraswamy adds, 'This vision of the beloved has no necessary relation to empirical reality. The beloved may be in every ethical sense of the word unworthy—and the consequences of this may be socially or ethically disastrous: but nevertheless the eye of love perceives her divine perfection and infinity, and is not deceived.' Coomaraswamy's words suggest his own uneasiness about the extreme democratic leanings of bhakti, and complex notions of worthiness.

In one poem Chandidas makes a statement that reminds Coomaraswamy of Nietzsche. It also probes forward to the Bauls, and carries enormous significance for Bengali poets of the modern period: 'Man is the greatest Truth of all. There is nothing beyond.'

> I throw ashes at all laws
> Made by man or god.

I am born alone,
With no companion.
What is the worth
Of your vile laws
That failed me
In love,
And left me with a fool,
A dumbskull?

My wretched fate
Is so designed
That he is absent
For whom I long.
I will set fire to this house
And go away.


Who was that girl?
Friend, who was that girl
Inflaming the river
With her fair skin? ...

The gold necklace
On the peaks of her breasts
Shone as the moon on the mountain snow.
The darkness in tears,
The shadows of the moon,
A flood of black hair rolled on her hips.
She rose from the river
Like a slice of the moon,
Glistening in twilight dark.
As I stood watching
And losing myself,
She walked away wringing and twisting my soul
Together with her sari—dripping, blue,
My heart still shivers in a fever of love ...

Danger grew
That evil day
As I held in my wide open eyes
Krishna.
I saw my life go.
Erupting with the fire of love,
My heart throbbed for nothing else
From that very day.

Water may kill a small fire
But how can I fight the holocaust
Of heart?
A burning forest rouses the world
Through flames,
But the embers of my heart
Ignite unseen ...


I never touch a black flower
In my diffidence.
Sadness grows.
I hear everywhere
Whispers about my dark love.

I never look at the sombre cloud
Fearing Krishna.
I do not wear kohl.
I screen my eyes
While going to the stream.
As I pass by
The *kadamba* shade,
I seal my ears
Hearing the flute.


I was pouring some water
That looked black
And I remembered Krishna.
In sleep and in dream

I constantly see
Only my Krishna.

I leave my black hair down,
I never dress it.
And I never wear black mascara in my eyes ...

I have blackened my golden skin
Longing for him,
Though he was not my husband.
I belonged to a respectable home.
As the fire encircled me,
My life began to wilt.
And my heart,
Brooding eternally,
Parched for my dark darling,
My Krishna ...

One gnawing pain is my home
And the other is Krishna.
Where else can I go,
O friend,
I have no ways open.
Life sizzling on fire
Singes my limbs,
And words of advice
Pour acid on my heart.
Like the death itself,
Krishna's love
is beyond remedy ...

My poor darling,
Your face seems hollow.
It hurts me to see
You adorned this way.
Your forehead, alas,

Is bruised by bracelets.
She must be wild
Who did this to you.
Your chest looks furrowed
With finger-nail scars,
Like red lotus-blooms
On a clear blue pool.
Who is that stone-girl
That harbours such ways?
Whoever taught her
This kind of loving?
It hurts me to see
Your eyes so damp.

Sit by me, darling,
I'll wipe your face clean.
You must be tired
of the sleepless night.


I have hardened my mind
Against the name of love.
Never again shall I hear of it.
If I ever do,
I shall instantly sacrifice
This miserable life.
I have no need of love.

In markets and riverbanks
Where people gather,
They call me a whore,
Loading my world with terrible shame.

Yet still, shame cools my heart,
I feel his presence
Like the southern breeze
On the lotus-pool ...

I want to forget
But I cannot forget him.
I do not see him
But I am devoted to him.
Even when I sleep
I repeat his name.
When I walk in the streets
I stare at the people
And I feel like crying
If they do not mention his name ...


She lingers out of doors.
She rushes in
And she rushes out,
her heart is restless.
Breathing fast,
She gazes at the *kadamba* wood.
What has happened
That she is not afraid?
The elders chatter
And the wicked gossip.

Is she possessed
By some enchanting god?
Forever restless
Careless of clothes,
Startled, she jumps in her dreams ...

Her desire inflamed
By passion and longing,
She reaches for the moon.

Chandidas says that she is caught
In the snare of Kaliya, the dark.


Like lightning in the clouds
She flashed away.

Her friends shadowing her
Melted in the space.
Never have I seen a girl as this:
Like patches of wild colour
Her ways were playful,
Eyes abyss deep.
Round her neck swayed a string of pearls.
Enchanted bees hummed at her fragrant skin.
Revealing and hiding her beautiful form
She walked away
Arm in arm with her friends.
Smiling a glance and looting my heart
She walked away.
Moonlight exploded on her glazed nails.
Her fatal eyes collected massacred lovers.
I lay unconscious with wounded heart,
My ribs cut open by her stabbing glance.

Chandidas says:
It is an absorbing tale
of an illness that does not end in the grave!


What have I gained
Saying Krishna and Krishna.
My heart is bruised raw,
Life simply sizzles
And I am dying of the fire of my mind.
In Gokula the town of the cowherds,
Nothing is forbidden!
They act as they wish.
The girls full of youth
Are ladies of homes.
Only Radha is the scandalous one!

Since the cruel god that created love
Made it dependent on the other's response,
I have no wish to live.
And I beg you not to name a girl Radha again.

Let us not talk of that fatal flute.
It calls a woman away from her home
And drags her by the hair to that Shyam.
A devoted wife forgets her spouse
To be drawn like a deer, thirsty and lost.
Even the wisest of ascetics lose their minds
And the plants and the trees delight in its sound.
What then can a helpless innocent girl do?


The morning crows and the *kokila* cried
The end of the night.
My lover was up and hastily left
Fixing his disheveled hair.
I cannot describe my suffering, O friend!
My dark lover left me saying not a word,
My heart was aching.
Resting in lassitude
My eyes were heavy,
As I discovered his clothes on me.

My people at home are eager to blame,
What can I do with his dress on me?

Chandidas says with a joyful heart,
Suffering leads to the treasure of love.


... Can anyone follow
the ways of my pain?
I live on the edge of a razor
that cuts me to shreds
as I move ...


Black poison burns me,
A dumb woman,
Married,
I live in a respectable home.

My heart wrapped in pain,
Speechlessly,
Secretly, chokes
As the flute grates my ears.
It lures my senses away
Leaving me my corpse.
It has no feeling for right or wrong.
The straight born reed
On the lips of that rogue
Has learned to be crooked.

Says Dwija Chandidas:
The company is wrong.
In the teeth of Rahu
The moon too turns black.


I have no idea
What made me lose my heart to Krishna,
This terrible love chokes me to death.
My world is intolerable
With rising heat,
My heart is stung
By a venomous snake.

Casting away
All ethics of castes
My heart dotes on Krishna
Day and night.
The custom of the clan
Is a far-away cry
And now I know
That love adheres wholly
To its own laws.


The essence of beauty
springs from the eternal play
of man as Krishna

and woman as Radha.
Devoted lovers
in the act of loving,
seek to reach
the goal.
Who is devoted
to whom and how
is of no interest.
Dedicate your soul
to the service of loving.
Love was born
to Radha
as one by one,
her eight friends helped.
If your senses
and the mind
can grasp the essence,
Krishna is reached.

Says Chandidas:
Listen, O brother man,
Man is the greatest Truth
Of all,
Nothing beyond.

—*Translated by Deben Bhattacharya**

# Rami (Ramoni)

About two hundred years ago a manuscript surfaced—it has been des-
cribed by Susie Tharu and K. Lalita as 'a sheaf of poems'—containing verse
composed after the death of Chandidas. Based on the autobiographical

* Bhattacharya, Deben. 1969. *Love Songs of Chandidas: The Rebel Poet-Priest of Bengal.* New York: Grove Press.

elements in them, scholars attribute the poems to Rami, or Ramoni, the celebrated lover for whom Chandidas threw cinders on 'all laws of men or gods'. The poems recount Rami's wanderings from town to town looking for work, until she reached the village of Nanur and took up the job of scrubbing the grounds of the Bashula Devi temple. This was where she met Chandidas, the priest of the temple, and together they scandalized the village with a love affair. It was not just with the fact of their love—between a brahmin and a low-caste woman—but as Susie Tharu suggests, 'it was the intensity of their involvement that broke the sanctions at a far deeper level.' Chandidas was exiled, and Rami disgraced.

On the surface the two poems here do not explore spiritual, mystical, or explicitly devotional themes. However, knowing of Rami's intense involvement with Chandidas, the furious social criticism and passion boiling up in the poems require them to be seen in the light of bhakti. Bhakti has archaic roots in India—among them a belief that erotic love and spiritual ecstasy share a common source. In much Vaishnava devotion, sexual ecstasy brings the lovers into the presence of Radha and Krishna. One of Chandidas's lyrics affirms this:

> The essence of beauty
> springs from the eternal play
> of man as Krishna
> and woman as Radha.

The first poem here erupts from Rami's desolation and fury at Chandidas's death. The Nawab of Gaur had invited Chandidas to sing at his court, and his queen, the Begum, went into rapture at the poet's performance. An electric passion passed between the Begum and Chandidas, the deep sexual attraction evident to everybody present, and the Nawab was incensed. He had Chandidas bound across the spine of an elephant and beaten to death, forcing his wife to watch the torture. Rami—in attendance at the public display—watched the execution in horror, while Chandidas kept his gaze fixed on her as he died. The Begum was devastated, and shortly afterwards killed herself.

'Rami's verses are unlike other Vaishnava lyrics of the time which were often abstract and philosophical,' write Tharu and Lalita. They continue: 'These poems express directly the yearning of a woman in love. There is no attempt to be discreet or to hide her passion. She curses and rages and laments.' Until Rami's poems came to light, the account of Chandidas's death might have been considered legendary. Now that these poems have surfaced into history, the membrane dividing myth from fact seems thinner.

Where have you gone,
    my Chandidas, my friend,
Birds thirst without water,
    despair without rain.
What have you done,
    O heartless lord of Gaur?
Not knowing what it means to love,
    you slay my cherished one.
Lord of my heart, my Chandidas,
    why did you break
The vows you made
    and sing in court?
Now evil men and beasts come swarming round:
    heavens turn to hell.

Betrayed by you, I stand in shame;
    you've crushed my honor in your hands.
Once, heedless, untouched by Vasuli's threat,
    you told the court with pride
You'd leave a Brahmin home, you said,
    to love a washergirl.
Now, lashed to the elephant's back,
    you reach me with your eyes.
Why should the jealous king heed
    a washerwoman's cries?
Soul of my soul, how cruelly on your fainting limbs
    the heavy whip strikes and falls,
Cleave through my heart, and let me die
    with Chandidas, my love.

And then the queen fell on her knees,
    'Please stop, my lord'" she cried.

'His singing pierced me to the heart.
   No more of this, I plead.
Why must you thus destroy
   limbs made for love alone?
Free him, I beg of you, my lord,
   don't make love your toy.
O godless king, how could you know
   what love can mean?'
So spoke the queen, and then, her heart
   still fixed on Chandidas, she died.
Rami trembled, hearing her,
   and hastened to the place.
She threw herself at those queenly feet
   and wept the tears of death.

                    —*Translated by Malini Bhattacharya**


What can I say, friend?
   I don't have enough words!
Even as I weep when I tell you this story
   my accursed face breaks into laughter!
Can you imagine the cheek of the sinister men?


   They have stopped worshipping the Devi
   And have started tarnishing my reputation.


Let the thunderbolt crash on the heads of those
Who from their housetops shout abuse at good people
   I won't stay any longer in this land of injustice,
I'll go to a place where there are no hellhounds.

                    —*Translated by Sumanta Banerjee*[†]


* Tharu, Susie and K. Lalitas, (eds.) 1993. *Women Writing in India, Volume I: 600 BC to the Early Twentieth Century.* New Delhi: Oxford University Press.
   † Tharu, Susie and K. Lalitas, (eds.) 1993. *Women Writing in India, Volume I: 600 BC to the Early Twentieth Century.* New Delhi: Oxford University Press.

# Bauls of Bengal

The Bauls, sometimes called 'god's troubadours' or 'god's vagabonds', are a Bengali sect, mostly drawn from the rural labouring classes. They live in small household communities, often with an allegiance to a guru living in the vicinity or buried nearby. They have produced over several centuries about forty well-known singers, and hundreds of others. These singers refer to themselves as Madmen. Their particular madness is social not personal. It includes a complete disregard of social and religious convention. They especially reject caste and show contempt for the scripture-based religions valued by most Bengalis.

The term Baul first occurs in the Bengali written record around the fifteenth or sixteenth century. It probably derives from the Sanskrit *vatula*, 'mad, insane', literally 'affected by wind'. The root *va* means to blow, and connotes a whirlwind. Vatula has a secondary usage, 'intent', or 'entirely devoted to'. Another possibility is that it emerged from the Sanskrit *vyakula*, restless, disordered.

The Baul religion has typically appealed to rural people subject to institutionalized exclusion, or to those exploited or harassed because of low social standing. This means the Bauls move largely among the rural, the poor, and those deprived of education. The most celebrated of all Bauls, Lalon Phokir, once sang:

> What form does caste take?
> I've never seen it brother
> with these eyes of mine.

Central to Baul belief is that the presence of love in a person is what confers status or dignity, not affiliation with any particular creed or caste. They also insist that life should be enjoyed. Celibacy the Bauls find absurd, and the built-in hypocrisy of denying urges given to the body they find repugnant. Asceticism they consider a dry path, rejecting it for a path that is juicy (*rosik*, from Sanskrit *rasika*). Because the body-mind is the sole vehicle any of us can use for liberation, the juicy path follows the way of vitality and freshness, made outwardly apparent in singing and dancing. The core of Baul spiritual practice is a sexual mysticism, with elements drawn from archaic belief, tantra, and other left-hand practices. Troubadour singing is not germane to their spiritual life, but seems to have emerged as a way for some to earn a small livelihood, supplemented by agricultural work at home. Mostly it is the men who sing, their lyrics composed in local vernacular or village languages. Occasionally they sing of Radha and Krishna, though their focus remains on the *moner manus*, the man of the heart, the elusive inward self. A.K. Datta (1871) writes: 'I have scarcely heard one or two Bauls who did not agree. By enjoyment of desire they eventually come to pure love in their sadhana. Then they perceive the full *lila* [divine play] of Radha and Krishna.'

Rabindranth Tagore brought the Bauls to international attention with a 1925 lecture on them at Calcutta University. He said, '"The Man of the Heart", to the Baul, is like a divine instrument perfectly tuned. He gives impression to infinite truth in the music of life.'

From their lyrics, the Bauls seem to draw on many sources: aboriginal lore, the Vedas, yoga, tantra, Vaishnava devotion, and Islamic mysticism. The translator Deben Bhattacharya speaks of them 'discarding the system while accepting the faith'. Their rejection of official, organized, or systematic religion—or poetry for that matter—locates them in a worldwide underground of antinomian poets, fervently spiritual, with incendiary political beliefs.

Though the Baul image became popular in Bengal among the upper middle classes—as an affirmation of regional identity—many in India find it difficult to accept them as authentic spiritual devotees. They have been excluded from most discussions of bhakti, probably due to their extreme scepticism of orthodoxy. The Baul Madan sings,

The door of love bears many locks;
Scriptures and beads.

Compare William Blake's 'The Garden of Love', where the Chapel has 'Thou shalt not, writ over the door',

And priests in black gowns, were walking their rounds,
And binding with briars, my joys & desires.


Mad, mad,
we are all mad.

Why is this word
so derogatory then?
Diving deep into the heart's stream
you will find
that no one is better
than the one who is mad.

Some are mad after wealth
and others for glory.
Some go mad
with poverty,
others with aesthetic forms
and the flavors of feelings.
Some are madly in love.
And some of those who go mad
only laugh or cry.
The glamour of madness is great.

Mad, mad!
Madness does not grow
on the tree,
but only when
fake and fact
are meaningless,
and all, being equal,
are bittersweet.

*—Anonymous*

A tramp by nature and a beggar at that,
he lives a strange life, almost insane,
with values of his own which are contrary
to those of others.
His home being under a tree,
he moves from district to district
all the year round,
as a dancing beggar who owns nothing
    in the world
but a ragged patchwork quilt.

*—Anonymous*

Come if you wish to meet
the new man.
He has abandoned
his worldly possessions
for the beggar's sack
that hangs from his shoulder.
He speaks of Kali
even as he enters the Ganges.

Simple words can overcome
ignorance and disbelief:
Kali and Krishna are one.
The words may differ—
the meaning is precisely the same.
He who has broken
the barrier of words
has conquered limitations:
Allah or Jesus, Moses or Kali,
the rich or the poor,
sage or fool,
all are one and the same to him.

Lost in his thoughts,
to others he seems insane.
He opens his arms
to welcome the world,
calling all to the ferry boat
tied to the coast of life.

*—Anonymous*


If you wish to board an airplane
you must travel light,
to be safe from the danger of a crash.
You must renounce
your errors and inhibitions
and show your credentials at the airport.
Paying your fare of devotion to God,
you must give up

your worldly wealth
to buy a ticket for a seat.
The feet of your Master,
the airplane,
will take you to Vishnu's sphere
in less than an eyelid's wink ...

*—Anonymous (Tape-recorded in Varanasi, 1954;*
*Singer: Hariprasad Debnath)*


The essence of love
lies in carnal lust
bearing a deep secret.
Only lovers
can unravel it.

*—Chandidas Gosain*

Human limbs
are held together
by a pair of lotus blooms
growing in the
lower and upper regions
of the body.
But the lotuses
open and shut
as the sun
in the body
rises and sets.

On which of these blooms
is the full moon born,
and on which the darkest
night of the month?

On which of these lotuses
rests the total eclipse
of the sun
and the moon?

*—Chandidas Gosain*

My life is a little oil lamp
floating on the waves.
But from which landing-pier
did you set me afloat?
With darkness ahead of me
and darkness behind,
darkness overlaps my night,
while the necklace of waves
constantly rings me about.
The storm of the night
relentlessly flows
below the stars,
and the lamp is afloat
on the shoreless water—
for company.

—*Gangaram*


Release the sensation of taste
on your tongue.
Open the doors of feeling
for beloved Krishna,
the image of eternal love.
Nectar, showering
on the lotus of spontaneity,
runs down the stem
to be one with the water
where flowers lie.

Lust and love
and the erotic acts
are housed in one single place
where sorrows and joys
do not exist.

—*Haude Gosain*


The scriptures will teach you
no prayers for love.

Love's record remains
unsigned by sages.

*—Lalan*


The road to you is blocked
by temples and mosques.
I hear your call, my Lord,
but I cannot advance,
prophets and teachers
bar my way.

Since I would wish
to burn the world
with that which cools my limbs,
my devotion to unity
dies divided.

The door of love bears many locks;
scriptures and beads.

Madan, in tears,
dies of regret and pain.

*—Madan*


Brothers,
come along
if you wish to smoke
the hemp of love.
With mounting intoxication
dissolve the habits
of your settled home
and take shelter
in the lord of faith.

He who smokes
the hemp of love
is wholly unaffected
by the drug.

*—Panchanam*

Prepare your heart
day by day
till it is ready
for the rise of the full moon.
Then lay a trap
at the bottom of the river
to catch it.

—*Pulin*


My heart is eaten away
by the white ants of the mind.

—*Panja Shah*


Now is the time for you
to repeat the names
of Radha and Krishna
the gods of devoted love.

The central beam
of your life is down
and your time has gone.
Your cheeks are sunk
and your hair is slack,
dead as a mop of jute.
Now is the time to repeat
the names of Radha and Krishna.

A fading rainbow,
you balance on a stick,
bent as a letter of the alphabet,
knees and head together.
Your time has gone
and all for nothing.
Your teeth are missing
but your eyes,
through empty holes,
still frown from your brows.

—*Ramachandra*

Attested by your own heart,
O my Master,
lead me the right way
as you play the melody
on the lute.
The lute could never sing
on its own
without you to play it.

*—Anonymous*

*—Translated by Deben Bhattacharya*[*]

For contrast with Bhattacharya's versions, following are two literal translations by ethnomusicologist Charles Capwell, taken from his study *The Music of the Bauls of Bengal* (1986). The songs Capwell recorded and transcribed prove full of tantrik and yoga imagery, allusions to secret Baul spiritual practice, and numerous references to religious stories, mythic figures, and sacred locations. Much of this material he footnotes. Of the first song reproduced here, he remarks, 'This song is of the heyali (riddle) type; what exegesis I received from Yotin [the singer] I offer without much hope of unraveling the riddle completely.' The lyrics refer, among other possibilities, to the mystery of conception, as well as to the *adhor manus*, the 'elusive' or inner man. Both songs, if read without concern for hidden meanings, hold an eerie beauty, with clear connections to the upside-down speech (*ulatbamsi*) of Kabir, and are strikingly similar to international modernist movements such as surrealism and futurism.

One moon has touched the body of another;
    what shall we do, having thought of that?
The mother's birth is from the daughter's womb;
    what do you call her?

* Bhattacharya, Deben. 1999. *The Mirror of the Sky: Songs of the Bauls of Bengal.* Prescott, Arizona: Hohm Press.

There was a girl of three months;
  in nine months she conceived.
In eleven months there were three offspring;
  which one will the fakir take?

Sixteen arms, thirty-two heads;
  the child speaks within the womb.
Who are its mother and father?
  That's a question to be asked!

There is a room with no doors;
  there is a man who doesn't speak.
Who furnishes his food,
  who lights the evening lamp?

Lalon Shah, the fakir, says,
  'If the mother touches, the son dies.
'He to whom these words have meaning,
  to him, indeed, belongs fakirdom.'

                              (*Singer: Yotin Das*)


Drive the human-body-motor-car upon the road of *sadhona.**
Be informed of who is your mind-driver
  by the word of a true guru.

Two lights are at the front of the car;
  they are lit night and day; they don't go out.
A car with seven locks;
  keep alert, o mind, while driving.

Within the car are two conductors;
  there are also sixteen acquitted men within.
Each is absorbed in his own work
  and has no connection with anyone.

Hiramon says, 'I remember the feet of the guru;
  come and drive for me, now.

* *sadhana,* or spiritual practice

'I cannot drive your car any longer
in this material kingdom.'

*(Singer: Narayon Das Odhikari)*

*—Translated by Charles Capwell*

* Capwell, Charles. 1986. *The Music of the Bauls of Bengal.* Kent, Ohio: Kent State University Press.

# Sakta Poems

## Ramprasad Sen

Long regarded the premier poet of the goddess in Bengal, Ramprasad Sen is held in equal esteem as a bhakta, a poet, and as an adept in Tantric practices. He composed several lengthier song-cycles, but his fame rests on scores, or perhaps hundreds, of individual padas to the goddess. The goddess he sings to has many moods, a chilling range of guises or manifestations, numerous names, and she moves readily between charnel ground and the poet's own inner landscape. If you keep in mind her unpredictability, it is easiest to speak of this goddess as Kali, the Black Lady; or as one North American poet spoke of her, 'the Tooth Mother'. Ramprasad's songs have currency throughout Bengal. They have been recorded by famous singers, translated into various European languages, imitated by poets outside India, and popularized by modern-day pagans. They now belong to an international community.

As with many bhakti poets, no more than a thin gauze of historical fact clings to Ramprasad. A teeming literature has sprung up around him, and in the two hundred plus years since his death poems attributed to him continue to surface, all carrying the restive tone known as *nindastuti*—praise through bitter reproach. Other poets have complained to or petitioned their deity; none have devised a complete poetics based on this mix of outrage and temper.

Rachel Fell McDermott, the most recent scholar to survey the poet's legacy, writes:

In spite of the awe in which Ramprasad is held by Bengalis, very little is actually known about him. The first biography, by Isvarcandra Gupta, was not written until 1853, at least seventy years after his death, and the contents of this work are peppered with encomia and hearsay.

As for the poems, Gupta wrote:

Works of his which had been collected earlier have by now almost disappeared, because in those days people used to guard them carefully like some secret mantra, not showing them to anyone even at the cost of their lives, bringing them out at puja time to decorate with flowers and sandalwood paste, as some people still do today, and though we would have given all we had we were not able to obtain any of the verses. Hidden in this way they have become completely destroyed. Worms and other insects ate them, moisture decomposed them, fire burned them, they were used by the impotent as charms to secure beautiful women or long life ...

In this atmosphere, legends have issued like smoke through cracks in the ground. Poems attributed to Ramprasad keep appearing. Their tone remains consistent: complaint, truculence, distress, fitful rage, and irrational tantrum—childlike moods focused on a neglectful mother who evidently leaves her child unprotected and undernourished. Ramprasad's extreme vulnerability seems intended to provoke in the listener a return to emotions that are elemental and archaic, even infantile. Here, where the secrets of childhood twist in discomfort, deep in an archaic realm, is where the goddess appears. It may be that the symbols of Ramprasad's tantric poetry perform their work at psychic levels unreachable to adult concerns, and exert their greatest effect when the listener has been reduced to naked vulnerability.

The known facts of Ramprasad's life would fit into a matchbox. He was born in the village of Halisahar somewhere between 1718 and 1723. He may have served for a time as a clerk in a Calcutta merchant house, where he reputedly filled up his account ledgers with hymns to Kali. After leaving the regular workforce, he must have returned to Halisahar; his early biographer, Gupta, records him receiving a land grant in 1758 from the Maharaja who would become his patron, Krsnacandra Ray.

Ramprasad's death dates vary between 1762 and 1803, a perplexing range of forty-one years. There does exist an oil portrait, supposedly of the poet, by English painter Arthur William Devis, painted in the early 1790s. Though Ramprasad would have been in his early seventies, the portrait shows a youngish man wearing a twisted loincloth, his dreadlocks or braids longer than his body; he leans casually against a great banyan, and a worn votive stone depicting Vishnu and his two wives tilts among the tree's thick roots.

Two stories about Ramprasad stand out. The first tells how his Calcutta employer, discovering that Ramprasad was scrawling hymns to Kali in the margins of the account books, found either the poems so good or the poet's devotion so convincing, that he sent him home with a stipend to continue writing. The other recounts how Ramprasad vanished—as many bhakti poets did—in a self-willed act of devotion. At Kali Puja, on the day of the goddess's immersion in the river near Halisahar, Ramprasad carried the *murti* or image on his head into the waters. He submerged himself along with the goddess, and as he sank below the surface his *brahmarandra*—the aperture at the top of the skull where the spirit escapes—split open. He died singing the final lines of a poem:

Prasad says,
There's no doubt in my mind:
Daksinakali is extremely severe.
    Ma, oh Ma,
my life is over, done for;
I've paid You my fee.


I spent my days in fun,
Now, Time's up and I'm out of a job.
I used to go here and there making money,
Had brothers, friends, wife, and children
Who listened when I spoke. Now they scream at me
Just because I'm poor. Death's
Field man is going to sit by my pillow
Waiting to grab my hair, and my friends
And relations will stack up the bier,
Fill the pitcher, ready my shroud and say

So long to the old boy
In his holy man's get-up.
They'll shout Hari a few times,
Dump me on the pile and walk off.
That's it for old Ramprasad.
They'll wipe off the tears
And dig in for their supper.

Pitying Mother, do I worship You
Out of my own free will?
Nobody would
If it weren't for the terror
Of Death.

Where are You, then, Mother,
Whose strength was before
All other powers? Your name
Is the only freedom.

O Devi of the tripled gaze,
Who else has that strength?

Listen to this story, Mother Tara,
My house is a battlefield, nothing but a quarrel
Of cross purposes, Five Senses,
Mother, each with a different desire,
All wanting pleasure all the time.

I have been born in eight million forms
And now I'm born a man,
A funny figure in a world
Whose gift to us is a load of misery.

Mother, look at Ramprasad
Trying to live in this house
Whose master is driven crazy,
Beaten by the Six Tenants.

How many times, Mother, are you going
To trundle me on this wheel like a blind-
Folded ox grinding out oil? You've got me
Tied to this old trunk of a world, flogging me
On and on. What have I done to be forced to serve
These Six Oily Dealers, the Passions?
All these births—eighty times 100,000—
As beast and bird and still the door
Of the womb is no more shut on me
And I come out hurting once more!
When a child cries out, calling the precious name
Of mother, then a mother takes it in her arms.
Everywhere I look I see that's the rule,
Except for me. All some sinners need to do
Is shout 'Durga' and—pouf!—they're saved.

Take this blindfold off so I can see
The feet that give comfort. There are many
Bad children, but who ever heard
Of a bad mother?

There's only one hope
For Ramprasad, Mother—that in the end
He will be safe at Your feet.


Mother, tell me where I should stand
With no relations in this world?
The father loves a child loved
By the mother—that's well known.

But the Father who bears Stepmother
On His head—don't expect love from Him.
And if You aren't loving, why shouldn't I go
To Stepmother and if She takes me up
You won't see me around here anymore.

Ramprasad says: Mother,
It's right here in the Vedas and Tantras:

He who repeats
Your name is going to end up
With a beggar's bowl and a cast-off rug.


I'm not calling You
Anymore, crazy Kali.

You, only a girl, waving a big sword,
Went into battle and without a stitch.

And there's that pittance You gave me
Only to snatch it right back.

As for this half-wit son,
You spoiled him all right Mother.

Poor Ramprasad cries:
Look what You've done Mother—
Piled this old tub
Full of goods, then sunk it.


Does suffering scare me? O Mother,
Let me suffer in this world. Do I require more?
Suffering runs ahead of me and runs after me.
I carry it on my head and set up a stand
In a bazaar to peddle it.
I'm a poison worm, I thrive on poison.
I carry it wherever I go.

Prasad says: Mother, lift off my load.
I need a little rest. It's amazing!
Others brag about their happiness,
I brag about my suffering.


The dark Mother
Is flying a kite
In the world's fairground.

O, mind, see—you are up there
In the gusts of hope,
Payed out on the string of illusion,
Your frame strung together
Skeleton and pulse stuck on.

But the Maker overdid it,
Giving the kite too much ego
In the building,
Toughening the string with glue
And powdered glass.

So Mother, if out of a thousand kites
You lose one or two,
Laugh and clap.

Prasad says: that kite is going to take off
In the southern breeze,
And on the other shore
Of this ocean of lives
It will dive fast to its freedom.


You'll find Mother
In any house.

Do I dare say it in public?

She is Bhairavi with Shiva,
Durga with Her children,
Sita with Lakshmana.

She's mother, daughter, wife, sister—
Every woman close to you.

What more can Ramprasad say?
You work the rest out from these hints.


Why should I go to Kashi?
At Her feet you'll find it all—

Gaya, the Ganges, Kashi.
Meditating in my lotus heart
I float on blissful waters.
Her feet are red lotuses
Crammed with shrines
And Her name spoken
Consumes evil like a fire
In a pile of dry cotton.
If there is no head to worry,
You can't have a headache.

Everytime I hear about Gaya,
The offerings there, the good deeds
Recited, I laugh. I know Shiva
Has said that dying at Kashi saves.
But I know too that salvation
Always follows worship around
Like a slave, and what's this salvation
If it swallows the saved like water
In water? Sugar I love
But haven't the slightest desire
To merge with sugar.

Ramprasad says with amazement:
Grace and mercy in her wild hair—
Think of that
And all good things are yours.


That's it, Mother!
The play is done.
It's over, my Happy One.
I came into this world
To play, took the dust
Of this world and played,
And now, Daughter of High Places,
Suddenly I'm scared. Death is so near,
So serious. I think of those games

I played as a boy, and all that breath
Wasted in the pleasure of marriage
When it should have gone for prayer.

Ramprasad begs: Mother,
Old age has broken me—what do I do now?
Mother, teach this worshipper
Worship, plunge me
Into the saving waves.

*—Translated by Leonard Nathan and Clinton Seeley**


I'll die of this mental anguish.
My story is unbelievable;
what will people say
when they hear it?
The son of the World-Mother
is dying of hunger pangs!
The one You keep in happiness,
is he Your favorite child?
Am I so guilty
that I can't even get a little salt
with my spinach?
You called and called me,
took me on Your lap,
and then dashed my heart
on the ground!

Mother,
You have acted like a true mother;
people will praise You.


* Sen, Ramprasad. 1998. *Grace and Mercy in Her Wild Hair: Selected Poems to the Mother Goddess by Ramprasad Sen.* Translated by Leonard Nathan and Clinton Seeley. Foreword by Andrew Schelling. Prescott, Arizona: Hohm Press.

Black clouds have risen in my sky
and my mind my peacock
dances, prancing in joy.
Thundering 'Ma! Ma! Ma!'
    clouds clash
        bedecking mountains
        with lightning flashes—
            smiles of bliss.

There's no stopping me, no rest for me;
water rains from my eyes
    soothing my heart's thirsty bird.

After this life, there's the next
and so many still to come.

Not for me, says Ramprasad:
no more births, no more wombs.


Mind, how do you think you'll find Her?
You're crazy; your house is dark!
If you have no realization,
    can you catch the object of realization?
Mind, to the best of your ability
first bring yourself under control.
Otherwise, like the moon hiding at daybreak
She'll hide Herself in your small, dark room
    in a secret cupboard.

I couldn't see Her
looking through the six philosophies
or the Agamas, Nigamas, or *Tantrasara*;
but he who appreciates the flavor of devotion
lives in that home in bliss.
Thirsting for realization, that supreme yogi
    inside of you
meditates from age to age.
Once realization dawns, he'll catch hold of you
    like a magnet grabbing iron.

Prasad says, I worship that yogi as Mother.
Shall I break this pot in public?
Mind, understand through hints and gestures.


Wait a minute, Death,
let me shout to my Mother.
Let's see whether She shows up
in my hour of need.
Eventually you'll get me; why worry about it now?
It's not for nothing that I keep Tara's name
in an amulet at my neck.
Mahesvari is my queen, and I
a tenant in Her personal estate.
Sometimes I'm poor, sometimes rich, but I'm never late with the
    rent.
Prasad says, Such is Mother's play; can anyone understand it?
How can I get to the bottom of it
when even the Three-Eyed Lord could not?


Look here—
it's all the woman's play,
secret,
Her intentions Her own.
In the controversies over *saguna* and *nirguna,*
She breaks one lump of clay with another.
In all matters this woman is equally willing to help
    except when you really need Her.

Prasad says, Sit tight
and float on the raft on the Ocean of Becoming.
When the high tide comes, move upstream, and
when the waters ebb, go down.

—*Translated by Rachel Fell McDermott**


* Fell McDermott, Rachel. 2001. *Singing to the Goodess: Poems to Kali and Uma from Bengal.* New York: Oxford University Press.

# Kamalakanta Bhattacharya

In the period when the earliest Sakta poetry emerged, the one figure that stands beside Ramprasad Sen, whose poems are equally vivid, is Kamalakanta. Unlike Ramprasad's poems, which are impossible to attach to a historical person, it appears that manuscripts in Kamalakanta's own hand have survived. The dates given for him vary enormously, largely calculated according to the births, careers, and deaths of members of his patron's family. This patron was the zamindar, Maharajadhiraja Tejaschand. Though Kamalakanta's output of poetry seems relatively fixed, without a tangled web of additions, the details of his personal life are much harder to authenticate. Stories of his life parallel Ramprasad Sen's so closely that it is possible both poets have been swept up to fit archetypal legends.

Though Kamalakanta and Ramprasad appear recent in the history of bhakti, they represent a tradition that reaches deep into prehistory. Feminist scholars and archaeologists have unearthed evidence of goddess worship across Asia, the Near East, and Europe, dating from Neolithic times. In historical times, cults surrounding the goddess have been fiercely suppressed, or in some areas slyly replaced with masculine deities. Though Ramprasad and Kamalakanta stand as foundational figures in India's Sakta poetry, it is likely their emotional structure, their secret teachings, and the precise imagery of their verse, represent a resurgence of ancient lineages. American poet Gary Snyder has spoken of 'the great Paleolithic subculture' which periodically emerges across the planet and values the feminine powers—values them for their fecundity, closeness to the life of herbs and animals, sophisticated insight into the human psyche, and their freedom from organized religions. This great subculture would be the tradition to which Sakta poetry belongs.

Kamalakanta composed Vaishnava padas as well as songs to Kali, all of them published in the various editions of his poetry, which first appeared in 1857. Early in the twentieth century, the Bangiya Sahitya Parishad dispatched workers throughout the Bengali countryside to locate and attempt to preserve disintegrating manuscripts. In 1918 one of these searchers, Prabodhchandra Chattopadhyay, visited the village of Canna Gram—a village linked by story with Kamalakanta. There he

borrowed from a temple curator a handwritten manuscript that proved
to be a Tantric manual, 'signed' by Kamalakanta (though copied down
by a scribe, whose name also appears).

Even without that manual it should be clear: like Ramprasad Sen's
lyrics, much in the poetry of Kamalakanta is coded with Tantric teachings.
While the songs are devotional—and full of nindastuti or 'praise in the
guise of complaint'—they also carry symbolic images about the arousing
of *kundalini*, and the significance of the chakras and *nadis* in the body.
This suggests that seemingly external references in the poems, or in the
stories or legends about Kamalakanta's life, could comprise an inward,
psychic language. His tantric manual, *Sadhak Ranjan*, centres on Siva,
'the Three-Eyed' patron of Tantra (and Kali's husband or lover). It
concludes with the lines:

My name is Kamalakanta. I think on Trilocana.
*Sadhak Ranjan* has been written with a heap of words.

Who is this enchantress
lighting up the war field
by Her black beauty?
Whose woman
   with huge eyes
   and a dreadful face
adorns Herself for battle
with a garland of heads?

Jackals are dancing
among the corpses and noncorpses,
making horrid noises. Joining them
She cackles aloud
   a hideous laughter
and places Her feet
on the heart of corpse-like Siva,
   tousling her long
      thick hair.

Kamalakanta stares
   absorbed
not even blinking his eyes.

So, forgetful Mahadeva,
You have fallen in love!


You got Her footprints
and now there's no separating You;
staring, staring,
You worship Her.
Her heavy locks of hair,
darker than a mass of clouds,
fall disheveled over her body.
      Incomparably glamorous!
Who knows the greatness of either of You—
      You sky-clad sixteen-year-old,
            and You, naked Tripurari?

There is no end
to the bliss of Madana's Bewitcher.
Lying lazily under the woman's hold,
He thirsts for the taste of love play.
Saying endearing things
He makes love to the beautiful one
      in the lotus heart of Kamalakanta.


Who is this,
dressed like a crazy woman,
robed with the sky?
Whom does she belong to?
She has let down Her hair,
thrown off Her clothes,
strung human hands around Her waist,
and taken a sword in Her hand.
Her face sparkles
from the reflection of Her teeth,
and Her tongue lolls out.
The smile on that moon-face drips
heaps and heaps of nectar.

Mother,
are you going to rescue Kamalakanta
in *this* outfit?


Ever-blissful Kali,
Bewitcher of the Destructive Lord,
Mother—
for Your own amusement
You dance,
clapping your hands.

You with the moon on Your forehead,
really You are primordial, eternal, void.
When there was no world, Mother,
where did You get that garland of skulls?

You alone are the operator,
we Your instruments, moving as You direct.
Where You place us, we stand;
the words You give us, we speak.

Restless Kamalakanta says, rebukingly:
You grabbed Your sword, All-Destroyer,
and now You've cut down evil *and* good.


From now on,
Don't deprive me any more, Tara.
Look, the danger of death is near.
What You've done to me is appropriate.
I endured, it endured.
But now I must think:
what is the recourse for a wretched man?
Death is not conquered,
But I am not afraid;
I only worry lest I forget Your name
at my going.

Even though Kamalakanta is in pain,
he will smile.
Otherwise people will say
You haven't given me any happiness,
Syama.


How will you rescue me, Tara?
There's only one of You,
but there are so many plaintiffs
I can't even count them!
You thought that because of my devotion
You could save me
     by hook or by crook,
but the devotion of a nondevotee
is like a conch-shell marriage bracelet
on the arm of a slut. It's true
     there is nothing more important
     than the name of Brahman
but even that is a great burden for me.
My mind and my tongue think alike
only at mealtimes.

Kamalakanta's Kali!
I'll tell you how to save me:
     sit in my heart.
The only worthwhile solution
is for You to keep watch.


Crazy Mind,
you haven't been able to recognize
what a treasure Kali is.
Just eating, sleeping, and having fun,
you waste your time, you crazy one.
You came into the marketplace of this world
hoping to trade.
What will happen now?

You seem to have lost your capital.
Through past merits you got a human body,
but what have you done about all those things
you had hoped to accomplish?

Kamalakanta's Mind!
Why have you come to this?
You're drowning in your own evil deeds,
and you're pulling me down as well.


Stay within yourself, Mind;
don't go into anyone else's room.
You will get what you need right here;
search in your own inner chamber.

Cintamani is like a philosopher's stone,
that greatest treasure
able to bring countless riches:
Her front door is strewn about
with so many jewels.

Going on pilgrimage
is a journey of sorrow, Mind.
Don't be too eager.
Bathe in the three streams of bliss.
Why not be cooled at their source,
your bottommost mystic center?

What are you looking at, Kamalakanta?
This world is full of false magic.
But you fail to recognize the magician—
and She's dwelling in your own body!


External rituals mean nothing
when the Goddess Filled with Brahman
is roused in your heart.
If you think on the Unthinkable,

will anything else come to mind?
It's like unmarried girls
with their various amusements;
when they unite with their husbands,
where are those games?
What will you worship Her with?
Everything is full of her essence.

And look at degenerate Kamalakanta!
She has made even him
a storehouse of good qualities.

—*Translated by Rachel Fell McDermott**

# Modern Sakta Poetry

The tradition of singing to goddess Kali has continued in Bengal into contemporary times. Internationally a resurgence of goddess awareness has brought Kali renown among neo-pagans and feminist groups, scholars and museum curators. Possibly it has been the suppression of goddess cults through much of history that has allowed her to reemerge with such vitality in modern times: a cultural return of the repressed. She continues to be depicted in traditional form, dancing in a charnel ground surrounded by her minions, while corpses burn and jackals feed on the leftovers. Often she performs her archaic dance on the corpse of Siva, who lies ash-coloured and inert, but with erect phallus, under her feet. This image, ghastly to those unschooled in its hidden meanings, holds precise philosophical and tantric instruction.

In eastern India the social or political charge of bhakti, long focused on the goddess, has kept regional concerns of justice in the popular eye. During India's twentieth century drive for Independence from Britain,

* McDermott, Rachel Fell. 2001. *Singing to the Goddess: Poems to Kali and Uma from Bengal.* New York: Oxford University Press.

the great goddess and Mother India became merged in popular culture and in the lyrics of nationalist singers: *Bande Mataram!* Sometimes—as with Najrul Islam (1898–1976), a Muslim who composed devotional hymns—the charnel ground Kali dances on becomes emblematic of an embattled, impoverished India. Toxic spills, nuclear waste, chemical discharges into air and water, increasingly find their cogent image in Kali's burning grounds.

Curiously, the Sakta tradition has produced few renowned women bhaktas, but there are some. Of the following poets, Ma Basanti Cakrabartti and Tarini Debi are female. Information about the lives of these modern bhaktas is hard to locate.

> Wherever there's a woman in any Bengali home
>    doing her work
>    screening her smiles with her veil
> she is You, Ma;
> she is You, Black Goddess.

> Carefully rising with the light of dawn
>    to attend with softened hands
>       to household chores,
> she is You, Ma;
> she is You, Black Goddess.

> The woman who gives alms, makes vows, does worship, reads scripture
>    all correctly and with a smile
> who drapes her sari over the child on her lap
> soothing its hunger with a lullaby,
> she is You, Ma;
> she is You, Black Goddess.

> She can't be anyone else;
> mother, father, sister, housewife,
>    all are You.
> Even at death
> smiling
> You make the journey with us.

My mind knows this, and my heart as well:
she is you, Ma;
she is You, black Goddess.

—*Ma Basanti Cakrabartti*


Let's be girls, Ma,
and play with dolls;
   come into my playroom.
I will take the Mother's role, so I can
teach You how.

If You make one dull or wretched,
hold him to Your bosom;
who else will ease his pain?
One who gets no jewels and gems, Ma,
at least should get his mother.

Some will be quite naughty,
others lie about inside their homes,
but all play games of hide-and-seek
   (our world here has no death, Ma)
crying as they leave at night, returning with the morning.

This little boy,
   you made him cry
     You made him fear.
     Now love away his fear,
   cease to make him cry—

or casting You aside
he'll run away.

When the play is finished
lull him into sleep;
   hold him in Your arms.

—*Najrul Islam*


Out of love for You
I have put aside my passions.

You're a brazen woman
    making love in the dominant position.
You've got no shame, no clothes,
and Your hair flies all over the place.
It is You, All-Destroyer,
who sets fire to creation.
I smear my body
with the ash from those cinders
    that disgrace.

In the eye of time
passion is a fleeting illusion.
It rises on Tuesday and sets on Saturday.
Dimram investigates these things and puts his passions aside.
Let me stand at Your feet, Ma,
the only place that truly exists.

—*Dimram*

Tara, this is why I call on You
    lest Siva's words prove to be false
    and you trick me at the end.
Siva says in the Tantras
that if one takes Tara's name one will be liberated.
So why am I still fallen in this world?

Tarini Brahmani says,
Listen, Bhavani,
at the end
    let me see those red feet.

—*Tarini Debi*

Ma, the mail train is leaving now;
    it's time for it to go.
But I have no 'ticket'
    and no credit,
        says the 'Rail Babu'.
Without money I can't even

exit through the gate. So I guess
they'll tie up my hands,
and I'll sit on the 'platform',
     branded by the 'Guard Babu's' blows.

But when I listen inside
it seems someone is speaking in my ear:
'Why bother with a "ticket"? Show your "pass";
     rely on the strength of the name.'
That's why at the end time
when destiny knocks
I'll speak that name
     and get a 'first class' seat;
the 'Checker Babu' will go away
confounded.

                              —*Kalyankumar Mukhopadhyay*


Tell me, what are you doing now, Mind,
sitting there with a blind eye?
There's someone in your own house
but you're so oblivious
you've never noticed!
There's a secret path
with a small room at the end—
and what an amazing sight inside:
caskets filled with jewels
that you never even knew about.
There's a lot of coming and going along that path.
Go, upstairs, to the highest room,
and you'll see the moon rising.

Premik says excitedly,
Keep your eyes open;
if you want to be awake in yoga
you must travel this secret way.

                              —*Mahendranath Bhattacarya*

Wait a moment, Death;
let me sing aloud to the Mother
and grace my eyes
with the sight of Her red feet.

The Great Lord Himself, Forgetful Siva,
lies at my Mother's feet,
    She the Greatest Power
        the universe
        moving and still.
That's why I drape myself
in Kali's name, printed
on a cloth.

Death replies,
Oh devoted one, does Ma belong to you alone?
I am also the Mother's child.
But where to get Her vision?
Today I wish the same as you:
    to rest in Her embrace.

—*Tapas Ray*
—*Translated by Rachel Fell McDermott* *

* McDermott, Rachel Fell. 2001. *Singing to the Goddess: Poems to Kali and Uma from Bengal.* New York: Oxford University Press.

# Finale

## Bhanusimha (Rabindranath Tagore)

Late in 1875, the eminent Calcutta journal *Bharata* published eight poems by a previously undiscovered, seventeenth-century Vaishnava poet, Bhanusimha. The language of the poems was Brajabuli, a Bengali literary vernacular that had gone unused for centuries and had been almost exclusively used by Vaishnava poets. Over the following six years *Bharata* published five more poems attributed to Bhanusimha. Only gradually did it emerge that Bhanusimha had never existed. Who had written these lyrics? Likely the poems were the work of a young man from a renowned and eccentric artistic family, who claimed he had found the manuscript in the Calcutta library of the Brahmo Samaj: Rabindranath Tagore. Tagore had been fourteen when he published the first Bhanusimha poems. The name Bhanu Singha (as Tagore anglicized the name in his memoirs) plays on his own name. Bhanu and Rabi both mean 'sun'. Singha and Tagore (Sanskrit: *thakkura*), each hold a secondary meaning: 'chief; man of rank'.

Was this a literary hoax? A brief biographical account of Bhanusimha published by Tagore in 1884 proved a bitingly sardonic parody of western scholarship, and of the slavish imitation of that sort of scholarship by Indian scholars. The essay presented outlandish evidence for absurd possibilities: 'Therefore it has been proved beyond all doubt that Bhanusimha took birth on or about AD 438 or 6000 BC. If anyone can refute this we shall regard them as our dearest friend, for our goal is nothing other than to ascertain the truth.'

As Tagore's reputation grew over the decades, and as he lost the need for angry parodies or youthful derision of the *panditas*, he did not abandon the poems as juvenilia. Instead, he added to them, tinkered with their emotions and imagery, and was still working on a set of twenty-two poems—the eventual number—in the year of his death, 1941. Some fierce instinct made the Bhanusimha poems nearly his first, as well as his last—seventy years in the making.

Many worlds meet in these poems. There is the eastern Indian and Bengali tradition of song cycles dedicated to the love of Radha and Krishna, a tradition begun by Jayadeva in the twelfth century, adopted by Vidyapati, Chandidas, and numerous other vernacular poets from the fifteenth century onwards. The love of Radha and Krishna is a theme often adopted in esoteric terms by the rural Bauls, a tradition Tagore admired. But the Bhanusimha poems are no less the earnest, youthful work of India's preeminent Modernist poet. It's worth noting the Modernist (even postmodern) interest in literary pseudonyms, the elaborate Dadaist hoax, as well as the Ethnopoetics project of unearthing ancient poetries (real or imaginary) to rejuvenate contemporary verse. Finally, there is the old, well-documented tradition of poets developing a persona through possession by a god, a spirit power, a witness to supernatural events, or by some other unaccountable force.

No doubt the invention of (or possession by?) a female persona permitted Tagore to explore ways of speaking to which he might otherwise not have gotten access. His friend and contemporary William Butler Yeats found such an opening, late in life, with the poems of 'Words for Music Perhaps', and the unforgettable figure of Crazy Jane. The entire history of Bengali Vaishnava poetry from Chandidas onwards would devise poems spoken in the voice of Radha or a female messenger. That Tagore kept to his Bhanusimha poems—and his female voices wrapped inside a male persona—from age fourteen until his eightieth year, suggests that whatever the original impulse, the poems are no simple ruse. They went to the core of his emotional and spiritual life, and perhaps to the core of the life he envisioned for a post-colonial India. His translator Tony Stewart writes:

Tagore's fascination with the Bhanu songs suggests that they were anything but juvenilia; they stand apart in his vast corpus as his most frequently revised works. The mythical setting of the songs is one familiar to any Bengali speaker, yet their content—especially the looming presence of death in the latter poems—violates the Vaisnava expectations on which they depend.

It is violation of tradition that has always made bhakti poetry fresh and irrefutable. Tagore's Vaishnava poems look forward more than they look backward, and give new, complex twists to a tradition that is built on subversion, outspokenness, and shifting approaches to authorship. The tangled web of persona within persona, of seriousness within pseudonym or hoax, makes these lyrics simultaneously the most backward looking and the most modern of Tagore's work.

1

*Spring at last! The amuyas flare,*
*half-opened, trembling with bees.*
*A river of shadow flows through the grove.*
*I'm thrilled, dear trusted friend,*
*shocked by this pleasure-flame—*
*am I not a flame in his eyes?*
*His absence tears at me—*
*love blooms, and then spring*
*blows the petals from the world.*
*In my heart's grove the cuckoos pour out*
*a bewildering fountain of pleasure-drops,*
*jewels of the universe.*
*Even the bee-opened flowers mock me:*
*'Where's your lover, Radha?*
*Does he sleep without you*
*on this scented night of spring?'*

I know he breathes secrets to you—
I can see their perfumes still dispersing
among the leaves of your longing.
Have I no memory of my own?
Besides, your head is full of flowers.
Go wait for him in the last shreds

of your innocence, crazy girl,
until grief comes for you.

3

*He never came to me.*
*In the whole long dark he never came*
*to tend my lacerated heart.*   •
*I'm a girl with nothing, a tree*
*with neither flowers nor fruit.*

Go home, poor tragedy. Distract yourself
with chores, dry your eyes. Go on now,
dear tattered garland, limp with shame.

*How can I bear this staggering weight?*
*I'm budding and blooming at once,*
*and dying, too, crushed by thirst*
*and the leaves' incessant rustling.*
*I need his eyes in mine, their altar's gold fire.*
*Don't lie to me. I'm lost in that blaze.*
*My heart waits, fierce and alone.*
*He'll leave me. If he leaves me, I'll poison myself.*

He drinks at love's fountain too,
my friend. His own thirst will call him.
Listen to Bhanu: a man's love
whets itself on absence if it's true.

4

That jewel-dark blue becomes you, Lord,
and rules your heart.
Radha sits alone and inconsolable as night
wrenches into dawn. Through veils of tears
she stares into the Yamuna's starry nothingness,
crazed by grief, by crickets.
She walks, she sits, she throws herself down
beneath the banyan, in the tryst-shadows,

a twig in her tangled hair. She cries
at a faraway flute, and leaves the floor unswept.

> *You're cruel, Lord of the lonely dark,*
> *so far away in Mathura.*
> *In whose bed do you sleep?*
> *Who slakes your thirst upon waking?*
> *Where are your sun-colored clothes—*
> *lost among the trees? And your crooked smile?*
> *Whose necklace gleams on your neck?*
> *Where have you thrown my wildflower chain?*
> *My golden love for whom I bloom unseen,*
> *you rule my emptiness, my endless nights.*

For shame, black-hearted one—
you're coming with me.
That girl is suffering.

7

> *Listen, can you hear it?*
> *His bamboo flute speaks*
> *the pure language of love.*
> *The moon enlightens the trees,*
> *the path, the sinuous Yamuna.*
> *Oblivious of the jasmine's scent*
> *I stagger around,*
> *disheveled heart bereft of modesty,*
> *eyes wet with nerves and delight.*
> *Tell me, dear friend, say it aloud:*
> *is he not my own Dark Lord Syama?*
> *Is it not my name his flute pours*
> *into the empty evening?*

> *For eons I longed for God,*
> *I yearned to know him.*
> *That's why he has come to me now,*
> *deep emerald Lord of my breath.*
> *O Syama, whenever your faraway flute thrills*

*through the dark, I say your name,*
*only your name, and will my body to dissolve*
*in the luminous Yamuna.*

Go to her, Lord, go now.
What's stopping you?
The earth drowns in sleep.
Let's go. I'll walk with you.

## 10

*Your flute plays the exact notes of my pain.*
*It toys with me.*
*Where did you learn such stealth,*
*such subtle wounding, Kan?*
*The arrows in my breast*
*burn even in rain and wind.*
*Wasted moments pulse around me,*
*wishes and desires, departing happiness—*
*Master, my soul scorches.*
*I think you can see its heat in my eyes,*
*its intensity and cruelty. So let me drown*
*in the cool and consuming Yamuna,*
*or slake my desire in your cool,*
*consoling, changing-moon face.*
*It's the face I'll see in death.*
*Here's my wish and pledge:*
*that the same moon will spill its white pollen*
*down through the roof of flowers*
*into the grove, where I'll consecrate my life*
*to it forever, and be its flute-breath,*
*the perfume that hangs upon the air,*
*making all the young girls melancholy.*
*That's my prayer.*

Oh, the two of you, way out of earshot.
If you look back you'll see me, Bhanu,
warming herself at the weak embers of the past.

## 12

*I know who visits your dream, Dark One.*
*Say her name. Her smile streaks*
*like lightning through clouds of sleep.*
*Syama, she has nothing with which to repay you.*

*Such impatience, bihanga!*
*Don't wake my sleeping Syama.*
*And you, moon, pour down your cold milk*
*on the sun's too early fire.*

Sometimes time is cruel in miniature,
as when dawn crowds the last hours.

## 14

*When we're together, nights like this delight me.*
*But when the clouds come down between us*
*and thrash around so rudely in the trees,*
*then I fear, Lord, imagining your breath-taking words*
*lost out there among the swords of lightning.*
*Come, you're drenched, Madhava,*
*drenched again, in these incessant rains.*
*Through the war of weather you've come to me.*
*Take off your clothes. Let me dry you. I'll untie my hair.*
*Come lie with me among the stalks of lotus,*
*skin cold and thrilled.*

He's the whole dark ocean of love.
And for the sake of love,
each being shall burn its own small flame.

## 18

*How long must I go on waiting*
*under the secretive awning of the trees?*
*When will he call the long notes of my name*
*with his flute: Radha, Radha, so full of desire*
*that all the little cowherd-girls will start awake*

*and come looking for him, as I look for him.*
*Will he not come to me,*
*playing the song of Radha with his hands and eyes?*
*He will not, Yamuna.*
*I have one moon—Syama—*
*but a hundred Radhas yearn for moonlight at his feet.*
*I'll go to the grove, companion river.*
*Alone, I'll honor our trysting-place.*
*No one will make me renounce it.*

Come with me into the dark trees.
You'll have your tryst,
its trembling rapture and its tears.

19

*You resemble my Dark Lord Syama,*
*Death, with your red mouth*
*and unkempt hair, dressed in cloud.*
*Sheltered in your lap, my pain abates.*
*You are the fountain of nectar, Death,*
*of immortality. I say aloud*
*the perfect word of your name.*
*Madhava has forgotten Radha.*
*But you, Dark Lord, accomplice,*
*you will not abandon me.*
*Call me now. I'll come into your arms*
*in tears, but soon lapse into half-closed sleep,*
*drowsy with bliss, my pain erased.*
*You won't forget me.*
*I hear a flute from the distant playgrounds,*
*the city far away—it must be yours,*
*for it plays my name.*

*Now darkness comes on, and with it a storm.*
*Clouds roil, and lightning slashes at the palms;*
*the desolate path twists into darkness.*
*I'm fearless now. I'll meet you there, Death,*
*in the old trysting-place. I know the way.*

Shame on your faithlessness, Radha.
Death is not another name for love.
You'll learn for yourself.

## 22

*I've fallen from my life, friend—*
*my tears since birth have washed my charms away.*
*But I've known pure love.*
*If I glimpse for an instant*
*my own Dark Lord on the forest path,*
*I kiss the dust at his feet a hundred times,*
*as if each grain were a jewel.*

*Unlucky, star-crossed birth.*
*I long to stay within the shadow*
*of his flute and taste from afar his dark smile.*

*Radha is the Dark Lord's Mistress!*
*May her pleasure be endless!*

*But it's grief that's endless,*
*a river of unseen tears.*

Is your indifference endless also, Black One?
Its half-bloomed flowers fall unseen
into the river of human tears.

*—Translated by Tony K. Stewart and Chase Twichell**

* Tagore Rabindranath. 2003. *The Lover of God.* Translated by Tony K. Stewart and Chase Twichell. Port Townsend: Copper Canyon Press.

# Appendix

## Statements on Poetry

How can you be praised in elaborate language,
similes, conceits, overtones, secondary meanings,
or textures of sound? They cannot contain
your form.

I never think of asking you to give me things,
so if you don't care for my poetry
I'll bear that alright.
It's only my tongue's natural work,
nothing other than my worship.

—*Dhurjati*[*]

[*] Heifetz, Hank and Velcheru Narayana Rao. 1987. *For the Lord of the Animals—Poems from the Telugu*. Berkeley: University of California Press.

Oh mother of mine,
There's ink* on my hands,
ink on my face.
The neighbors laugh.
My education amounts to nothing—
I see 'ShyaMa' in the letter M
And Kali in the letter K,
I dance and clap my hands.
Only my tears multiply
when my eyes light
on the rows of black marks
in multiplication tables.
I couldn't care less for
the alphabet's shades of sound
since your dark, lovely shade
isn't among them.
But Mother, I can read
all that you write
on leaves in the forest,
on the waters of the sea,
and in the ledger of the sky.
Let them call me illiterate.

—*Kazi Najrul Islam,*
*translated by Sagaree Sengupta*[†]

Make of my body the beam of a lute
  of my head the sounding gourd
  of my nerves the string
  of my fingers the plucking rods.

---

* The Bengali original plays on the word for ink, *kali*, pronounced identically with the name of the goddess Kali.

† Shaner, Lynne and Nancy Eickel (ed). 1999. *Devi: The Great Goddess.* Smithsonian Institution, Washington, D.C..

Clutch me close
  and play your thirty-two songs
  O lord of the meeting rivers!

                            —*Basavanna,*
               *translated by A.K. Ramanujan*[*]

In each glorious lotus
  *muladhara, svadhisthana, manipura* at the navel,
  *anahata,* and *visuddha*
You incarnate as letters
  v to s, b to l, d to ph, k to th,
    sixteen vowels at the throat
      and h and ks between the eyebrows.
My teacher was firm with me;
he told me to think of You like this in my body.

                       —*Ramprasad Sen,*
          *translated by Rachel McDermott*[†]

They [the Bauls] say, all these scriptures are nothing but leftovers from ancient celebrations. What are we, dogs?—that we should lick these leftovers? If there is need, we shall make new celebrations. By the grace of God, ever new sustenance will come. The truth of truths is their faith; however long the Word is needed, for so long will the Word arrive ever renewed—there will never be want. Having lost their faith, men, like dogs, collect together the left-over leaves [*pat*: leaf of banana or other plant used as a plate; leaf of palm used for book pages]. Even dogs one day abandon the leaves. Men are still more despicable. Their pride is showing which among the leaves is oldest!

                       —*Kshitimohan Sen,*
          *quoted in Charles Capwell*[‡]

[*] Ramanujan, A.K. 1973. *Speaking of Siva*. Baltimore; Penguin Books.

[†] McDermott, Rachel Fell. 2001. *Singing to the Goddess: Poems to Kali and Uma from Bengal*. New York: Oxford University Press.

[‡] Capwell, Charles. 1986. *The Music of the Bauls of Bengal*. Kent, Ohio: Kent State University Press.

I've burned my own house down,
the torch is in my hand.
Now I'll burn down the house of anyone
who wants to follow me.

—*Kabir,*
*translated by Charlotte Vaudeville**

---

* Vaudeville, Charlotte. 1974. *Kabir.* London: Oxford University Press.

# Glossary

**abhang**   a form of lyric used by the Varkari poets of Maharashtra

**amrita**   'deathless' (Greek: ambrosia). The juice of immortality, generally conceived as a nectar or fluid

**anchal**   border or edge of a woman's garment

**ankita**   a line used by the Virasaiva poets of Tamil Nadu in each of their poems, a 'signature' phrase—generally the name of their personal deity—which announces the poem's author

**Avatara** (Sanskrit) **avatar** (Hindi)   literally 'descended', an incarnation or appearance on earth of a deity in a particular form. Applied especially to Vishnu when he descends as Krishna, Rama, or another of his twelve *avataras*

**Bai**   'sister'. Suffixed to the names of many west and north Indian women *bhaktas*

**bhakta**   term for a spiritual devotee. Widely and generically used for someone who has dedicated their entire life to worship of a deity, guru, or formless principal (*nirguna*) of reality

**bhanita**  Bengali, signature line; the formal poetic phrase in which the poet interjects his or her own name or some identifying term. The *bhanita* can summarize the poem, comment ironically on it, or serve as a refrain joining songs of a cycle in oral performance. See **ankita** and **mudra**

**cintamani**  mind-jewel. Term used in yoga and tantra for the treasure of spiritual wakening

**chap**  stamp or seal. The poet's name or a recognizable phrase including the name, that testifies to the poem's authenticity. With the *chap* a bhakti poet validates or completes the poem. John Stratton Hawley: 'these seals make their poems *affidavits in verse*.'

**Das** (Sanskrit, **Dasa**) or *f.* **Dasi**  servant or slave. Often taken as a title by a devotee, e.g., Surdas or Tulsidas

**devadasi**  temple dancer; a woman dedicated to service in the temples, often the holder of rigorous training that is both ritual and artistic

**drakshyati vakshyati ramsyate**  'she will look ... speak ... take pleasure ...' (from Jayadeva's *Gita-govinda*)

**dukula**  cloth fine raiment, often used in sash, belt, or bodice, made from the inner bark of the *dukula* plant

**Govinda**  chief of cowherds. Epithet for Krishna, and the name that gives Jayadeva's Sanskrit *Gita-govinda* its title

**kadamba**  a type of tree, dark leafed with yellow blossoms, identified with Krishna. In iconographic art the tree signifies the god's presence. Botanical names: *Anthrocephalus cadamba* and *Nauclea cadamba*, both common on the Indian subcontinent. An ancient dynasty of Kannada took its name from the tree, and an early written script is also called *kadamba*.

**Kamadeva**  passion; desire. Personified as the love god; armed with a bow and arrows tipped with five flowers, he slips noiselessly among us. Also known as Ananga (Bodiless)

**Kamini**  (feminine) lover, passionate lady; more esoterically, a 'devotee of desire', or one devoted to love of the spirit

**kirtan** a religious group singing session, typically with a leader who recounts some narrative or sings the stanzas, with refrains sung by a full assembly

**kunja** a flower grove

**Madhava** Honeyed One, epithet of Krishna

**mudra (mudrika)** Sanskrit and north Indian, 'seal', sign, badge, emblem. In bhakti poetry, the signature the poet sets into the poem itself, generally his or her own name, or a stock phrase containing the poet's name. In the Tamil tradition the poet's signature was generally a name of the deity, referred to as the *ankita*. See also **bhanita, chap**

**Nanda** Krishna's foster father, a village headman among the cowherds. The mysterious opening of Jayadeva's *Gita-govinda* has him giving a directive, *nidesita*, to Radha.

**nirguna** without form. Scholars apply this term to the type of bhakti that does not envision a figurative deity, a god with qualities or attributes (*guna*). The 'eastern' Kabir is one of the principal examples of *nirguna bhakti*. Though he may use the name Ram, he refers not to Rama, the avatara of Vishnu, nor to another mythic figure, but to an inconceivable reality beyond description. Nirguna bhakti poets of north India are generally termed *sants*.

**pada; padam** a nearly pan-Indian term for a lyric composition. Often used interchangeably for poem, song, lyric. More specialized terms such as *bandish* mean something like composition, and refer specifically to the words. Also see **vacana**.

**Padmavati** the lotus-foot goddess, a name for one of Visnu's wives. Possibly the name of Jayadeva's own lover, used by him in the *Gita-govinda* as an epithet for Radha.

**Pandharpur** small town in Maharashtra, on the banks of the Chandrabhaga. Site of the central temple of Vitthal or Vithoba. Here the legendary bhakta Pundalik devoted himself to serving his elderly parents. This aroused the curiosity of Vishnu, who descended from his celestial home in Vaikuntha. Pundalik asked Vishnu to wait while he attended to his elderly parents, and gave the god a brick to stand on. He forgot Vishnu however, so fixed was he on assisting his elders. Vishnu was so impressed by the acts of devotion that he resolved to remain at Pandharpur for twenty-eight eons, waiting while his devoted followers traveled to visit him. A stone image stands in the temple, hands on hips, feet squarely fixed on a brick. This is the brick Pundalik asked Vishnu to wait upon.

**Pandurang** 'White One' ordinarily an epithet for Siva, but in Pandharpur an epithet of **Vishnu**. See Vithoba. Vithoba appears to have joined in himself attributes of both Vishnu and Siva.

**Rahu** a demon—or the severed head of a demon—that eats the moon repeatedly, causing its phases

**rasa** originally sap, juice, nectar, semen; the essence of life. In poetry and the arts, 'flavour' or taste of an emotion, the essence of an artistic mood. Traditionally poets recognized eight distinct rasas, with *sringara* or love the pre-eminent. More colloquially *rasa* can mean the essence of any experience.

**sadhana** (Sanskrit) spiritual practice

**saguna** a figurative deity, visually conceived, possessing attributes or *guna*, for example Krishna the cowherd, or Siva the blue-throated yogin. Saguna is one of the two forms or approaches to bhakti, the other being **nirguna**. Some poets seem able to balance both approaches without disharmony.

**sakhi** originally Sanskrit, meaning friend, intimate companion, and in that sense 'witness' (to someone's passions or travails). In northern bhakti traditions, *sakhi* refers to couplets or aphorisms that are pithy— the poet's witness to truth.

**samadhi** (Sanskrit) meditation, in which the mind is concentrated intensely upon an object. It comes to refer to any state of trance, and eventually gets specified as that final 'trance' by which a yogin or yogini departs from earthly existence. From this final meaning, it takes on a more concrete meaning: the site of that departure, hence 'tomb' or 'cenotaph'.

**sant** generic term for a saint or poet-saint, applied specifically to the nirguna bhaktas of Northern India. The term gets applied more loosely to holy men or women across the subcontinent, even if they conceive of their sadhana as working with a saguna or figurative deity.

**Sri** (Sanskrit) commonly a term of respect: mister or sir. Regularly used as an honorific for a deity, male or female: Sri Krishna, Sri Lakshmi. In Jayadeva's *Gita-govinda*, Sri is a feminine epithet for Radha or one of Vishnu's wives, 'Glorious'. Applied to humans it can be a high honorific, or simply mean "mister." Its feminine form in this case would be Srimati (abbr. Smt.).

**sri** (Telugu) spider; *Srikalahastrisvara*, 'the god of the spider, snake, and elephant', of whom Dhurjati sings

**tamala** dark-barked, white-blossomed tree, *Xanthochymus pictorius*. Tamala trees form the grove where Krishna and Radha consummate their love, and as with the **kadamba** has become for artists and poets an emblem of Krishna.

**tribhanga** three bends or 'bent in three', a traditional stance in iconography or dance traditions, with a bend at neck and hip

**Trilocana** Three-eyed. Epithet of Siva

**vacana** saying; poetic composition. Used particularly for the southern traditions. The emphasis is on speech—these are to be spoken, not simply heard (*sruti*) or remembered (*smriti*).

**Varkari** pilgrim or traveller. Term used for the religious tradition and its poet-saints of Maharashtra, who hope at least once in their lives to make the pilgrimage to Pandharpur (or Pandhari) where the image of Vithoba resides. The earliest of these poets, their 'archmentor and preceptor' (Dilip Chitre) was Jnanadeva, born in 1275. The Varkaris had a huge number of followers, transcending caste and gender barriers. Many of them fiercely and stridently opposed brahmanic Hinduism and Sanskrit scriptural authority. Until the close of the seventeenth century the Varkaris were the principal force in Marathi literature, laying the ground for the literatures that would follow.

**Vithoba**    a form of Vishnu worshipped by the Maharashtrian Varkari poets. His principal temple sits in the city of Pandharpur, and his devotees try to make a pilgrimage to the temple once in their lives. Also known as **Vitthal** or **Pandurang**

**Vitthal**    affectionate name for Vithoba

# Bibliography

Alston, A.J. 1980. *The Devotional Poems of Mirabai.* Delhi: Motilal Banarsidass.

Bhattacharya, Deben. 1969. *Love Songs of Chandidas: The Rebel Poet-Priest of Bengal.* New York: Grove Press.

———— 1970. *Love Songs of Vidyapati.* Edited by W.G. Archer. New York: Grove Press.

———— 1999. *The Mirror of the Sky: Songs of the Bauls of Bengal.* Prescott, Arizona: Hohm Press.

Bly, Robert. 2004. *Kabir: Ecstatic Poems.* Boston: Beacon Press.

Bly, Robert and Jane Hirshfield. 2004. *Mirabai: Ecstatic Poems.* Boston: Beacon Press.

Capwell, Charles. 1986. *The Music of the Bauls of Bengal.* Kent, Ohio: Kent State University Press.

Chitre, Dilip. 2003. *Says Tuka – 1: Selected Poems of Tukaram.* Pune: Sontheimer Cultural Association.

———— 2008. 'Ahimsa, Bhakti and Saintliness in Politics: Mahatma Gandhi's Continuation of a Uniquely Indian Tradition'. Unpublished lecture.

———— 2008: *Poets of Vithoba: Anthology of Marathi Bhakti Poetry.* Unpublished manuscript.

Chitre, Dilip. nd. 'The Practice of Marathi Poetry: A Survey of Seven Centuries of Interruptions'. Unpublished manuscript.

Coomaraswamy, Ananda K. 1913. *Thirty Indian Songs*. London: Olde Bourne Press.

———— 1927 *The Dance of Shiva*. New York: The Sunwise Turn.

Dalrymple, William. 2004. 'The Song of the Holy Fools'. *The Guardian* Saturday, (7 February).

Dehejia, Vidya. 1990. *Antal and Her Path of Love: Poems of a Woman Saint from South India*. Albany, New York: State University of New York Press.

Dharwadker, Vinay. 2003. *Kabir, The Weaver's Son*. New Delhi: Penguin Books.

Dimock, Edward C., Jr. and Denise Levertov. 1967. *In Praise of Krishna: Songs from the Bengali*. Garden City, New York: Anchor Books.

Eliade, Mircea. 1958. *Yoga: Immortality and Freedom*. Translated from the French by Willard R. Trask. New York: Princeton University Press.

Elwin, Verrier. 1946. *Folk-Songs of Chattisgarh*. New Delhi: Oxford University Press.

Feldhaus, Anne (ed.) 1996. *Images of Women in Maharashtrian Literature and Religion*. Ithaca, New York: State University of New York Press.

Ginsberg, Allen. 1994. *Cosmopolitan Greetings: Poems 1986–1992*. New York: HarperCollins Publishers.

Goetz, Hermann. 1966. *Mira Bai, Her Life and Times*. Bombay: Bharitiya Vidya Bhavan.

Hawley, John Stratton and Mark Juergensmeyer. 1988. *Songs of the Saints of India*. New York: Oxford University Press.

Hawley, John Stratton. 2005. *Three Bhakti Voices: Mirabai, Surdas, and Kabir in Their Times and Ours*. New Delhi: Oxford University Press.

Heifetz, Hank and Velcheru Narayana Rao. 1987. *For the Lord of the Animals: Poems from the Telugu*. Berkeley: University of California Press.

Hess, Linda and Shukdev Singh. 2002. *The Bijak of Kabir*. New Delhi: Oxford University Press.

Hirshfield, Jane. 1994. *Women in Praise of the Sacred: 43 Centuries of Spiritual Poetry by Women.* New York: HarperCollins Publishers.

Jackson, William J. 1998. *Songs of Three Great South Indian Saints.* New Delhi: Oxford University Press.

Kaul, Jayalal. 1973. *Lal Ded.* New Delhi: Sahitya Akademi.

Lorenzen, David. 2004. 1991. *Kabir Legends and Ananta-Das's Kabir Parichai.* Albany, New York: State University of New York Press.

Lorenzen, David. 2004. 'Bhakti'. In Sushil Mittal and Gene Thursby *The Hindu World,* New York: Routledge.

*Manushi.* (ed.) 1989. Women Bhakta Poets, Nos. 50–52 (Jan–June), New Delhi.

McDermott, Rachel Fell. 2001. *Singing to the Goddess: Poems to Kali and Uma from Bengal.* New York: Oxford University Press.

———— 2001. *Mother of My Heart, Daughter of My Dreams: Kali and Uma in the Devotional Poetry of Bengal.* New York: Oxford University Press.

Miller, Barbara Stoller. 1977. *Love Song of the Dark Lord: The Gitagovinda of Jayadeva.* New York: Columbia University Press.

Mokashi-Punekar, Rohini. 2002. *On the Threshold: Songs of Chokhamela.* New Delhi: The Book Review Literary Trust.

Monier-Williams, Sir M. 1899. *Sanskrit-English Dictionary.* Revised edition. New York: Oxford University Press.

Mookerjee, Ajit. 1975. *Yoga Art.* New York Graphic Society.

Pound, Ezra. 1963. *Translations.* New York: New Directions.

Ramanujan, A.K. 1973. *Speaking of Siva.* Baltimore; Penguin Books.

———— 1981. *Hymns for the Drowning: Poems for Visnu by Nammalvar.* Princeton, New Jersey: Princeton University Press.

———— 1985. *Poems of Love and War, from the Eight Anthologies and the Ten Long Poems of Classical Tamil.* New York: Columbia University Press.

Ramanujan, A.K., Velcheru Narayana Rao, and David Shulman. 1994. *When God is a Customer: Telugu Courtesan Songs by Ksetrayya and Others.* Berkeley: University of California Press.

Rao, Velcheru Narayana and David Shulman (trans). 2005. *God on the Hill: Temple Poems from Tiruppati.* New Delhi: Oxford University Press.

Rothenberg, Jerome. 1985. *Technicians of the Sacred: A Range of Poetries from Africa, America, Asia, Europe & Oceania.* Berkeley: University of California Press.

Rothenberg, Jerome. 1986. *Pre-Faces & Other Writings.* New York: New Directions.

Sargeant, Winthrop. 1984. *The Bhagavad-Gita.* Albany, New York: State University of New York Press.

Schelling, Andrew. 1993. *For Love of the Dark One; Songs of Mirabai.* Illustrated by Mayumi Oda. Boston: Shambhala Publications.

———— 2003. *Wild Form, Savage Grammar: Poetry, Ecology, Asia.* Albuquerque, New Mexico: La Alameda Press.

———— 2007. *Kamini: A Cycle of Poems from Jayadeva's Gita-govinda.* St. Louis: emdash studios.

Sen, Ramprasad. 1998. *Grace and Mercy in Her Wild Hair: Selected Poems to the Mother Goddess by Ramprasad Sen.* Translated by Leonard Nathan and Clinton Seeley. Foreword by Andrew Schelling. Prescott, Arizona: Hohm Press.

Shaner, Lynne and Nancy Eickel (ed.) 1999. *Devi: The Great Goddess.* Smithsonian Institution, Washington, D.C..

Snyder, Gary. 1969. *Earth House Hold.* New York: New Directions.

———— 1968. *The Back Country.* New York: New Directions.

Tagore, Rabindranath. 2003. *The Lover of God.* Translated by Tony K. Stewart and Chase Twichell. Port Townsend: Copper Canyon Press.

Tedlock, Dennis. 1978. *Finding the Center: Narrative Poetry of the Zuni Indians.* University of Nebraska Press.

Tharu, Susie and K. Lalita (eds.) 1993. *Women Writing in India, Volume I: 600 BC to the Early Twentieth Century.* New Delhi: Oxford University Press.

Thiel-Horstmann, Monika. 1983. *Crossing the Ocean of Existence: Braj Bhasa Religious Poetry from Rajasthan.* Wiesbaden: Otto Harrasowitz.

Vaudeville, Charlotte. 1974. *Kabir.* London: Oxford University Press.

# Translators

SUMANTA BANERJEE's translations have appeared in *Women Writing in India, Vol. I: 600 B.C. to the early twentieth century,* edited by Susie Tharu and K. Lalita.

DEBEN BHATTACHARYA (1921–2001) was a renowned musicologist, filmmaker, and writer. His translations of Bengali poets and singers into English were for many years the most influential volumes available. He made field recordings of music throughout Bengal, bringing the classical and folk music of India to England and the United States. Bhattacharya divided his time between Calcutta and Paris until his death in 2001.

ROBERT BLY, born in 1926 in the state of Minnesota, has been a controversial poet and counterculture leader since 1966 when he founded American Writers against the Vietnam War. Through the nineteen-fifties, sixties, and seventies, he edited poetry journals committed to translation and an internationalist view of literature. Bly remains one of North America's most visible poets and translators.

CHARLES CAPWELL is a former editor of the journal *Ethnomusicology* and is faculty at the University of Illinois. He is the author of *The Music of the Bauls of Bengal.* Capwell plays the sitar and teaches Hindustani music.

DILIP CHITRE (1938–2009) was one of the foremost writers and critics of post-Independence India. He wrote in both Marathi and English, and translated extensively from the Varkari tradition, notably the complete poems of Tuka Ram in three volumes. Also a painter and filmmaker, Chitre helped found the journal *Shabda* in 1954, and served as honorary editor of the journal *New Quest* until his death in 2009.

ANANDA K. COOMARASWAMY (1877–1947), born in Colombo, Sri Lanka, moved to England as a young man. His many writings on Indian art, philosophy, metaphysics, poetry, and music were among the first serious studies available to the West. After relocating to the United States in 1917 he moved in avant-garde circles in New York and Boston. Coomaraswamy served as Keeper of Indian Art at the Boston Museum of Fine Arts, the first such exhibit in North America, much of it developed out of his own personal collection.

SUSAN DANIELS's translations have appeared in *Women Writing in India, Vol. I: 600 B.C. to the early twentieth century,* edited by Susie Tharu and K. Lalita.

VIDYA DEHJIA is an art historian and curator. With training in Tamil and Sanskrit, as well as several modern Indian languages, she serves as a professor of Indian art at Columbia University. Her publications and exhibits range in content from early Buddhist art, to Chola Dynasty bronzes, to photography.

EDWARD C. DIMOCK, JR. (1930–2001) was professor emeritus in South Asian languages and literatures at the University of Chicago. He traveled to Calcutta in 1955 and is remembered as a father figure to the generation of American scholars who studied in India after World War II. Dimock wrote and translated extensively from the Bengali. In 1992, the Indian government awarded Dimock its highest honorary degree, Desikottama, for lifetime achievement.

ANNE FELDHAUS is a professor of religious studies at Arizona State University. She works on the religious traditions of the Marathi-language region of western India, and specializes in folk Hinduism and religious geography.

KALI MOHAN GHOSE (1884–1940) was a co-founder of the London Brahmo Samaj in 1912, along with Rabindranath Tagore and William Rothenstein. In London he met the American poet Ezra Pound and their Kabir translations helped introduce the great *bhakta* poet to England. Ghose later became a lawyer of the Kolkata High Court.

JOHN STRATTON HAWLEY joined the faculty at Barnard College, Columbia University in 1986, where he is a professor of religion. He is the author or editor of fifteen books, most of them treating of Hinduism and the religions of India, including the recent study, *Three Bhakti Voices: Mirabai, Surdas, and Kabir in Their Times and Ours.*

HANK HEIFETZ is an independent American poet, student of Sanskrit, and translator, who collaborates with South Asian scholars on volumes of early Indian poetry. He has published translations of Kalidasa's *Kumarasambhava*, Tamil songs of war and wisdom with George Hart, and versions of Durjati with V. Narayana Rao.

LINDA HESS teaches in Stanford University's Department of Religious Studies. Specializing in Hinduism, she writes on the poetry of North India's great 15th-and 16th-century bhakta poets, their popularity and influence, and the modes in which their work is performed.

WILLIAM J. JACKSON, a scholar of Telugu, is author of *Songs of Three Great Indian Saints*, published by Oxford University Press, Delhi.

MARK JURGENSMEYER is director of the Orfalea Center for Global and International Studies and affiliate professor of religious studies at the University of California, Santa Barbara. He is an expert on religious violence, conflict resolution, and South Asian religion and politics. Jurgensmeyer has published more than two hundred articles and twenty books.

DENISE LEVERTOV (1923–1997) was born and published her first poetry in England. In 1948 she relocated to the United States, becoming one of the preeminent members of 'the new American poets', the post World War II generation of experimentalists. Levertov was a staunch anti-war activist. Her commitment to 'organic form' in poetry—rather than the use of received forms—remains influential. Her best known titles appeared during the Vietnam war, including *Life in the Forest* and *Relearning the Alphabet*.

RACHEL FELL MCDERMOTT teaches at Barnard College in New York City. She has published numerous books on goddess worship in Bengal, translated the renowned Shakta poets, and recently co-edited two volumes, *Encountering Kali: In the Margins, at the Center, in the West* and *Breaking Boundaries with the Goddess: New Directions in the Study of Shaktism*.

LEONARD NATHAN (1924–2007) was a poet, critic, and professor of rhetoric at the University of California, Berkeley. He collaborated on translations from many languages, notably with the Nobel Prize winning Polish poet Czeslaw Milosz. He learnt Sanskrit and produced a fine edition of Kalidasa's *Meghaduta*.

EZRA POUND (1885–1972), one of America's leading Modernist innovators, argued in his polemical essays for an international approach to literature. Among his many translations are the medieval Troubadors of Provence, Tang Dynasty Chinese poets, and the classic anthology of Confucius. His monumental poem *The Cantos* was a fifty-year project, still the most influential Modernist epic, and is credited with expanding the range of poetry—both in form and in subject matter—in unprecedented ways.

ROHINI MOKASHI-PUNEKAR teaches at the Indian Institute of Technology, Guwahati, in the Department of Humanities and Social Sciences. Her translations of Chokamela's songs, *On the Threshold*, is being released by Yale University Press in 2010.

A.K. RAMANUJAN (1929–1993) was a renowned poet, essayist, and translator from the languages of South India. He has been honoured with a volume in the Oxford India series. Among his translations are *Speaking of Siva*, two volumes of poetry by Namalvar, and a collection of classical Tamil verse, *Poems of Love and War*. He taught for many years at the University of Chicago.

VELCHERU NARAYANA RAO, professor of languages and cultures of Asia at Emory University, has had a lifelong connection to historical and contemporary Telugu literary movements. He has published anthologies of Tamil poetry, including *Twentieth Century Tamil Poetry*, and collaborated closely with American poets and scholars on numerous books.

VILAS SARANG, born in 1942 in Karwar, a tiny coastal town in the south of Maharashtra, is one of the significant modern Marathi writers. He has written short stories, poems, a novel, and influential pieces of criticism in his first language, Marathi, as well as in English. Sarang is avowedly anti-representational in his aesthetics, putting him at odds with diaspora and 'exiled' non-resident Indian-English writers such as Salman Rushdie and V.S. Naipaul.

ANDREW SCHELLING, born in 1953, teaches poetry, translation, and wilderness writing at Naropa University in Colorado. His poetry is known for its close engagement with the natural world. He has edited journals and anthologies including *The Wisdom Anthology of North American Buddhist Poetry*, and has published six volumes of translation from Sanskrit and other languages of India. *Dropping the Bow: Poems from Ancient India* received the Academy of American Poets translation prize.

CLIFTON SEELEY, born in 1941, is a scholar of Bengali language and literature. He studied at the University of Chicago and for his PhD dissertation wrote a biography of Jibanananda Das. Among writers he has translated are Ramprasad Sen, Buddhadeva Bhose, and Michael Madhusudan Dutt. Seeley also designs software for the Bengali language.

SAGAREE SENGUPTA is a poet, independent scholar, and translator. She teaches at Bates College in Lewiston, Maine.

DAVID SHULMAN is on the faculty of the Hebrew University of Jerusalem. He has written extensively on the history of religion in India, translated poetry from the Tamil and Telugu, and is a scholar of Carnatic music and Dravidian languages. He has also been active in Middle East politics, in particular around the Israeli–Palestinian conflicts.

SHUKDEV SINGH collaborated on translations of Kabir's *Bijak* with American scholar, Linda Hess.

TONY K. STEWART is a Bengali religion and literature specialist, currently an associate professor of South Asia religions at North Carolina State University. In collaboration with Edward C. Dimock, Jr. he has published a translation of the Bengali and Sanskrit hagiographies of Caitanya, entitled *Caitanya Caritamrta,* (Harvard Oriental Series, 1999).

CHASE TWICHELL, born in 1950 in New Haven, Connecticut, has lived for many years in the Adirondack Mountains of upper New York State. She is the author of numerous books of poetry, and her work typically reflects her commitment to Buddhist practice. She left a career of teaching to found Ausable Press, an enterprise dedicated to publishing poetry.

CHARLOTTE VAUDEVILLE, an internationally recognized scholar of medieval Indian literature and religion, is emeritus professor, University of Paris, Sorbonne-Nouvelle. She has published many scholarly volumes including *Myths, Saints and Legends in Medieval India* and *A Weaver Named Kabir.*

# Copyright Statement

- Kabir, translated by Ezra Pound, in Ezra Pound, 1963, *Translations*. New York: New Directions. Reprinted here with permission from Faber and Faber.
- Kabir, translated by Linda Hess and Shukdev Singh, in Linda Hess and Shukdev Singh, 2002, *The Bijak of Kabir*. New Delhi: Oxford University Press. Reprinted here with permission from Linda Hess.
- Kabir, translated by Robert Bly, in Robert Bly, 2004, *Kabir: Ecstatic Poems*. Boston: Beacon Press. Reprinted here with permission from Beacon Press.
- Ravidas (Raidas), Surdas, and Tulsidas, translated by John Hawley and Mark Juergensmeyer, in John Hawley and Mark Juergensmeyer, 1998, *Songs of the Saints of India*. New York: Oxford University Press. Reprinted here with permission from John Hawley and Mark Juergensmeyer.
- Mirabai, translated by Andrew Schelling, in Andrew Schelling, 1993, *For Love of the Dark One*; Songs of Mirabai. Illustrated by Mayumi Oda. Boston: Shambhala Publications. Reprinted here with permission from Hohm Press.
- Dadu Dayal, translated by Monika Thiel-Horstmann (revised by Andrew Schelling), in Monika Thiel-Horstmann, 1983, *Crossing the Ocean of Existence: Braj Bhasa Religious Poetry from Rajasthan*. Wiesbaden: Otto Harrasowitz. Reprinted here with permission from Otto Harrasowitz.

## EAST

- Jayadeva, translated by Andrew Schelling, in Andrew Schelling, 2007, *Kamini: A Cycle of Poems from Jayadeva's Gita-govinda*. St. Louis: emdash studios. Reprinted here with permission from Ken Botinick.
- Songs from the Bengali, translated by Edward C. Dimock Jr. and Denise Levertov, in Edward C. Dimock Jr. and Denise Levertov, 1967, *In Praise of Krishna: Songs from the Bengali*. Garden City, New York: Anchor Books. Reprinted here with permission from Random House.
- Vidyapati, translated by Deben Bhattacharya, in WG. Archer (ed.), 1970, *Love Songs of Vidyapati*. Reprinted here with permission from Deben Bhattacharya's heir.